THE POCKET fat, carbohydrate & fibre counter

Carol Bateman

p

This is a Parragon Book
First published in 2004

Parragon
Queen Street House
4 Queen Street
Bath BA1 1HE, UK

ISBN: 1-40544-658-7

Printed and bound in Indonesia

Nutrition Consultant: Stephanie Green, RD and Fiona Hunter

Photographer: Karen Thomas

Home Economist: Valerie Berry

NOTES

This symbol means the recipe is suitable for vegetarians

This book uses imperial metric or US cup measurements Follow the same units
of measurement throughout; do not mix imperial and metric

All spoon measurements are level: teaspoons are assumed to be 5 ml and
tablespoons are assumed to be 15 ml Unless otherwise stated eggs and indi
vidual vegetables such as potatoes are assumed to be medium and pepper is
freshly ground black pepper

Recipes using raw or very lightly cooked eggs should be avoided by infants the
elderly pregnant women convalescents and anyone suffering from an illness
Pregnant and breastfeeding women are advised to avoid eating peanuts and
peanut products

The times given are an approximate guide only Preparation times differ
according to the techniques used by different people and the cooking times
may also vary from those given Optional ingredients variations or serving sug
gestions have not been included in the calculations

Illustrations: Anna Hunter-Downing

Produced by the Bridgewater Book Company Ltd

CONTENTS

WHY A FAT, CARBOHYDRATE & FIBRE COUNTER?

Balancing the amounts of fat, carbohydrate and fibre we consume daily is vital to good health.

Your diet should provide all the energy, protein, vitamins and minerals you need to stay healthy and active every day, so enabling you to enjoy life to the full.

In our affluent Western society, however, it is very easy to choose a diet that is too high in fat, sugar and salt and too low in fibre, especially as our busy lifestyles often mean eating takeaways or ready-prepared foods. It is well known that a high-fat, high-sugar, high-salt diet may be harmful, leading to increased risk of coronary heart disease, high blood pressure and certain forms of cancer.

Choosing to eat sensibly is clearly vital to good health. Although there are no single 'good' or 'bad' foods, the key to better health is to select a balanced range of nutritious foods every day, and indulge in fattening or less nutritious 'treats' less often.

The Pocket Fat, Carbohydrate & Fibre Counter is designed to help you achieve this. It will enable you to understand the composition of a wide range of available foods and give you

the knowledge to select and balance your daily nutritional requirements and those of your family.

Dietary energy is measured in kilocalories (kcal) or kilojoules (kJ), which comes from three major food sources: protein, fat and carbohydrate. The daily number of calories (as they are more usually known) needed depends on your sex, age, weight and activity level.

While protein is essential for the growth and maintenance of body tissues, most adults eat more than enough. High-fibre foods such as bread and pulses also provide useful amounts of protein, so achieving your daily fibre target can mean that you also obtain your protein requirements.

The A–Z food listing focuses on counting three essential nutrition elements in the foods you choose: fat, carbohydrate and fibre. (Although fibre is not a nutrient it has a vital role in keeping the gut active and healthy.)

If you follow the recommendations for your daily intake you will also obtain the optimum protein, vitamins and minerals essential for good health.

The most useful foods are highest in carbohydrate and fibre – so aim to limit the fats and choose starchy, not sugary (low-fibre), carbohydrates.

Your diet need not meet strict daily targets. Balance too much fat one day with less the next. Overall, try to achieve a healthy diet and remember that eating should be enjoyed!

THE FOOD PYRAMID

This diagram shows the recommended balance of the five different food groups in your daily diet. The largest group is the starchy carbohydrates, followed by fruit and vegetables. Protein and dairy foods are next, with the smallest group containing the fatty and sugary foods. Around half the total calories you need should come from the starchy carbohydrates and 33–35 per cent from fats.

Foods containing fat, foods containing sugar
Eat only small amounts of these foods

Milk and dairy foods
Consume in moderation

Meat, fish and alternatives
Limit to 15–20% of
daily energy

*Fruit and vegetables (high
in fibre, low in calories)*
Aim for 5 helpings a day

Starchy carbohydrates – bread, other cereals and potatoes
Should provide 45–50% of daily energy

Bread, other cereals and potatoes

This group includes all the low-fat, starchy carbohydrate foods, such as bread, rolls, chapatis, breakfast cereals, oats, pasta, noodles, rice, beans, lentils, plantain, green bananas and dishes made from maize, millet and cornmeal. Most of these foods are good sources of dietary fibre and contain other vital nutrients. For good health the aim should be to have 45–50% of your daily energy (calories) from this food group.

Fruit and vegetables

This includes all fresh, frozen and canned fruit and vegetables, salad vegetables, beans and lentils and can also include some dried fruit and fruit juice. Try to choose a wide variety of fruit and vegetables – at least five portions every day – to get the vital vitamins, minerals and antioxidants they provide.

Milk and dairy foods

The dairy foods (milk, cheese, yogurt, fromage frais) are all good sources of protein and minerals, especially calcium. Low-fat dairy products retain the calcium content of full-fat kinds. If avoiding dairy products choose alternatives fortified with calcium.

Meat, fish and alternatives

This group includes red meats, such as beef, pork, bacon, lamb and meat products (e.g. sausages, beefburgers), also poultry, fish, fish products (e.g. fish fingers, fish cakes), offal (liver, kidney, heart), eggs, beans and lentils, nuts and nut products, textured vegetable protein and other meat alternatives. Only small amounts of these high protein foods are needed.

Foods containing fat, foods containing sugar

This includes butter, margarine, low-fat spreads, cooking oils, mayonnaise and oily salad dressings, biscuits, cakes, puddings, ice cream, chocolate, sweets, crisps, sugar and sweetened drinks. Try to limit your intake of fatty and sugary foods. The natural sugar in fruit, vegetables and milk is not harmful to health – but the aim is to limit added sugar.

USING THE COUNTER

The A–Z food counter lists the carbohydrate, fibre and fat content in grams per weight/average serving of food. If the food has no typical serving, a 100 g amount is given.

Everyone's fat and carbohydrate requirements differ slightly depending on their individual daily energy (calorie) needs. A normal-weight female aged 19–50 needs around 1900 calories per day, while a normal-weight male of 19–50 needs around 2500 calories. Follow these guides or estimate your own daily calorie count using the calculation on page 10.

FAT

All fats contain a mixture of fatty acids: saturated, monounsaturated and polyunsaturated. While the kind of fat we eat can make a difference, all types are equally high in calories. Fat in food may be visible (e.g. butter, oil) or invisible (e.g. cheese, meat).

Dietary fat raises cholesterol in the bloodstream. High blood cholesterol increases the risk of coronary heart disease and other medical conditions. Current advice states that the total daily fat intake should provide 33 per cent of the daily calories, of which no more than 10 per cent should come from saturated fats.

Saturated fats are believed to raise the level of the harmful LDL (Low Density Lipoprotein) cholesterol connected to heart disease.

Polyunsaturated fats reduce both HDL (High Density Lipoprotein) and LDL cholesterol. The omega-3 fatty acids (found in oily fish) may help to prevent clotting and reduce the risk of heart disease.

Monounsaturated fats raise the ratio of beneficial HDL to LDL cholesterol and may also have a protective role in the prevention of coronary heart disease.

COUNTING FAT

A woman who needs 1900 calories a day will require about 630 calories (33 per cent) to come from fats. If 1 gram fat = 9 calories, the desired fat intake would be 70 g/day. A man using 2500 calories needs no more than 95 g fat.

CARBOHYDRATE

Carbohydrates comprise starchy and sugary foods. Staple foods worldwide, such as bread, rice, potatoes, millet, pasta, cassava, yam, plantains and green bananas, are starchy carbohydrates. High-protein beans, lentils, seeds and nuts also contain starchy carbohydrates.

Natural sugars are present in milk and many plant foods, especially fruit. Concentrated or pure sugars, occurring in honey and cane/beet sugars are high in calories, but of little nutritional value.

COUNTING CARBOHYDRATES

A recommended 50 per cent of daily energy should come from carbohydrates (with the least from pure sugars) but 45 per cent is acceptable. At a rate of 4 kcal/g this works out at 215 g daily (based on 1900 calories) or 280 g daily (based on 2500 calories).

FIBRE

This is the fibrous part of plant foods (cereals, fruit, vegetables, pulses, nuts, seeds) that remains in the intestine after digestion. Fibre helps prevent constipation, coronary heart disease, gall bladder disease and some cancers. The recommended intake of dietary fibre is an average of 18 g/day. To achieve this, eat plenty of bread, cereals and potatoes, as well as five portions of fruit and vegetables.

ENERGY & BODY WEIGHT

Are you the right weight for your height? There are charts available for you to check against or you can work out your body mass index (BMI). To do this, divide your weight (in kg) by your height (in metres squared):

30+	Obese – may harm your health
26–29	Overweight – losing weight is recommended
19–25	Normal – within the healthy range
~ 19	Possibly underweight – may harm your health

How much food energy you need each day varies according to your sex, age, weight and activity level. The following equations will give an estimate of your energy requirement, but remember, these are very general calculations.

1. Use the equation for your sex and age, and add in your weight in kg:

MEN

Age: 18–29: [(0.063 x weight) + 2.896] x 239

Age: 30–60: [(0.048 x weight) + 3.653] x 239

Age: Over 60: [(0.049 x weight) + 2.459] x 239

WOMEN

Age: 19–29: [(0.062 x weight) + 2.036] x 239

Age: 30–60: [(0.034 x weight) + 3.538] x 239

Age: Over 60: [(0.038 x weight) + 2.755] x 239

2. Although this gives you the basic calories you require, it does not include activity, so multiply the answer to equation 1 by your activity level.

First select the activity level for your job. A desk job will be 'light', but a more active job such as nursing will be at least 'moderate'. If you exercise regularly you will be moderately active, but if you exercise rarely your leisure activity level will be 'light'.

Leisure Activity	Occupational Activity		
	light	moderate	moderate/ heavy
	M F	M F	M F
Non-active	1.4 1.4	1.6 1.5	1.7 1.5
Moderately active	1.5 1.5	1.7 1.6	1.8 1.6
Very active	1.6 1.6	1.8 1.7	1.9 1.7

To lose weight, subtract about 500 cals from your daily requirement and use the counter to check your intake. Very low-calorie diets are not a good way to lose weight. By making this smaller adjustment you will lose weight more slowly, but have a better chance of long-term success.

Note: These guidelines are for adults only – children need a proportionately higher calorie intake.

FOOD LABELLING

Food labels provide information on the contents of cans, packs and wrappings and in many countries are also required to carry nutritional information. The contents are listed in order of the percentage of each ingredient, with the largest quantity appearing first. Use this listing to compare similar products for content and value.

Nutrition labelling is compulsory in many countries, but rules vary on what must appear on the label. Information is usually presented in quantities per 100 g, which is useful for comparing similar products. Information may also be given per portion, which may be helpful when planning a healthy diet.

The basic nutritional information found on all food labels in the UK is:

Energy	as kcal and kJ
protein	g
carbohydrate	g
fat	g

Although not mandatory, many foods are labelled more fully, for example:

energy	as kcal/kJ
protein	g
carbohydrate	g, *of which*
sugars	g
starch	g
fat	g, *of which*
saturates	g
monounsaturates	g
polyunsaturates	g
fibre	g
salt	g
sodium	g

For carbohydrates, the first figure given is the total amount of carbohydrate in the product. Giving information on sugars helps in choosing items with a lower sugar content.

Fats are presented as total fat in the product, and may also state how much is saturated. Information on saturates is helpful, because any fat that is not saturated will be mono- or polyunsaturated.

A

ALCOHOL

For many of us drinking alcohol is an enjoyable social activity. A glass of wine with a meal or a drink in the pub with friends is a pleasant way to relax at the end of the day.

Nutritional content

Alcohol is made from the yeast fermentation of different fruits or grains including grapes, hops, apples and barley. Spirits are distilled and contain no sugar, while beers and wines have varying amounts of sugar still remaining. Alcoholic beverages contain almost no nutritional value other than sugar but they do contain calories.

Medical benefits

In small amounts, alcoholic drinks such as red wine may protect against some medical conditions including coronary heart disease. However, too much alcohol may cause weight gain and is harmful to health.

Moderation

It is wise to keep your intake of alcohol to sensible levels. One way is to check how many units you consume on a regular basis. A single unit of alcohol equals:

½ pint of ordinary beer
1 small glass (60 ml/2oz) sherry or fortified wine
1 small glass (120 ml/4oz) wine
1 single measure of spirits.

Men can drink about 3–4 units a day or up to 28 units a week without harm to health. For women the level is lower, about 2–3 units per day or up to 21 units a week.

FOOD	FAT g	FIBRE g	CARB g	ENERGY kcal	kJ
++ known to be present but unmeasured					
0+ trace only present					
ALCOHOL					
BEER					
bitter, draught, 1 pint, 574 ml	0	0	13	172	712
bitter, low alcohol, 333 ml	0	0	7	43	180
brown ale, bottled, 1 pint, 574 ml	0	0	17	172	723
lager, alcohol-free, canned, 333 ml	0	0	5	23	103
lager, canned, 333 ml	0	0	0+	97	403
lager, low alcohol, canned, 333 ml	0	0	5	33	137
lager, premium, canned, 333 ml	0	0	8	196	813
pale ale, draught, 1 pint, 574 ml	0	0	12	161	677
shandy, canned, 333 ml	0	0	10	37	160
stout, canned, 333 ml	0	0	5	100	420
stout, strong, canned, 333 ml	0	0	15	120	509
strong ale/barley wine, 1 pint, 574 ml	0	0	35	379	1579
CIDER					
dry, draught, 1 pint, 574 ml	0	0	15	207	872
low alcohol, canned, 333 ml	0	0	12	57	246
sweet, draught, 1 pint, 574 ml	0	0	25	241	1010
LIQUEURS					
cream-based, 25 ml	4	0	6	81	338
egg-based, 25 ml	2	0	7	65	273
higher strength, (Curaçao, Drambuie), 25 ml	0	0	6	79	328
lower strength, (cherry brandy, coffee) 25 ml	0	0	8	66	275
SPIRITS					
brandy, gin, rum, whisky	0	0	0	56	230
alcohol 40% 25 ml					
alcohol 37.5%	0	0	0	52	215
WINES					
champagne, dry, 125 ml	0	0	2	95	394
port, 125 ml	0	0	15	196	819
red, dry, 125 ml	0	0	0.3	85	354
rosé, 125 ml	0	0	3	89	368
sherry, dry, 50 ml	0	0	1	58	241
sherry, medium, 50 ml	0	0	3	58	241

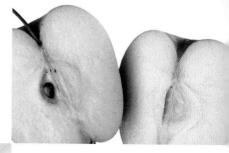

A

APPLES

Apples are a delicious and versatile food that can be used in many ways. They can be eaten raw as a crunchy snack or baked, cooked, made into sauce or purée and cooked in pies or cakes.

Nutritional content

Apples are a good source of fibre (about 2 g/apple) and vitamin C, which is stored close to the skin. When you peel an apple you lose about half the fibre and a significant amount of vitamin C. One apple contains about 10 g carbohydrate in the form of starch and natural sugar. Apples are not as high in vitamin C as citrus fruits.

However, if they are eaten frequently enough they can become a valuable source of this important vitamin.

A healthy snack

For most children apples are a favourite fruit. So, when children ask for a snack, give them an apple rather than a biscuit or crisps and remember that a crispy apple makes a delicious addition to a packed lunch.

FOOD	FAT g	FIBRE g	CARB g	ENERGY kcal	ENERGY kJ
(ALCOHOL)					
sherry, sweet, 50 ml	0	0	4	68	284
tonic wine, 100 ml	0	0	12	127	532
vermouth, dry, 1 measure, 48 ml	0	0	1	52	217
vermouth, sweet, 1 measure, 48 ml	0	0	8	72	303
white, dry, 125 ml	0	0	1	83	344
white, medium, 125 ml	0	0	4	93	385
white, sweet, 125 ml	0	0	7	118	493
white, sparkling, sweet, 125 ml	0	0	6	93	384
APPLE					
cooking, baked with sugar, 1, 150 g	0	4	29	111	477
cooking, baked without sugar (flesh only), 100 g	0.1	2.2	11	43	183
cooking, raw, peeled, 1, 100 g	0.1	2.2	9	34	150
cooking, raw, with skin & core, 100 g	0.1	1.6	6	27	109
cooking, cooked with sugar, 100 g	0	1.8	19	74	314
cooking, cooked without sugar, 100 g	0	2.0	8	33	138
eating, dried, 100 g	0.5	10	60	238	1014
eating, raw, unpeeled, 1 av.	0	2.4	14	56	239
eating, raw, peeled, 1 av.	0	1.8	11	45	190
juice, 100 ml	0	0+	10	38	164
APRICOT					
canned in juice, 140 g	0	1.7	12	48	206
canned in syrup, 140 g	0	1.7	23	88	375
dried, 100 g	0.7	22	43	188	802
dried, cooked with sugar, 100 g	0.3	8.5	22	92	393
dried, cooked without sugar, 100 g	0.3	8.9	18	77	328
raw, 3, 120 g	0	2.3	9	37	160
ready-to-eat, 100 g	0.6	18	37	158	674
cooked with sugar, 100 g (weight with stones)	0.1	1.7	17	67	88
cooked without sugar, 100 g (weight with stones)	0.1	1.5	6	25	108
ARTICHOKE					
globe, boiled, 220 g	0	++	3	18	75
Jerusalem, peeled, boiled, 100 g	0	++	11	41	207
ASPARAGUS					
boiled, 120 g	0.5	0.8	1	16	64
canned, 100 g	0.5	2.9	2	24	100

B

BABY FOODS

Milk from the breast or bottle is the only food a baby needs in the first weeks of life. Solid foods should not be introduced too early – preferably not before 6 months – but some hungry babies will need to start solids before others.

Fat and fibre

Babies and very small children need energy for growth and development. Fat provides a vital source and should not be restricted at this age. Babies also need fibre but not too much because they are unable to process it. However, do give fruit and vegetables to help prevent constipation.

Health warning

Do not give babies and small children nuts, particularly peanuts. They may suffer an allergic reaction or choking.

Solid foods

The first solid food given is often baby rice, mixed with the baby's usual milk, or puréed fruit or vegetables. Puréed foods can be frozen in an ice cube tray then one or two cubes reheated thoroughly when needed. Home-cooked food should be prepared without salt and spices. Retail baby foods are useful for days out or emergencies.

FOOD	FAT g	FIBRE g	CARB g	ENERGY kcal	kJ
AUBERGINE					
raw, 100 g	0.4	2.3	2	15	64
fried in oil, 100g	32	3	3	302	1262
AVOCADO					
raw, 1 av., 145 g	2.8	++	3	276	1137
BABY FOODS (RETAIL)					
apple & apricot cereal, dried, organic, 100 g	5.8	4.6	70	384	1840
apple & banana, jar, 100 g	0.2	1.5	14	60	256
apple & raspberry, dried, 100 g	4.5	5.6	70	374	1586
banana & apple puree, jar, 100 g	0.2	1.5	14	60	256
carrot & lamb, jar, 100 g	2.4	0.8	8	63	264
carrot & potato, organic, jar, 100 g	0.1	2.7	6	26	111
cheese & tomato bake, dried, 100 g	11.6	2.2	64	411	1718
cottage pie, jar, 100 g	2.8	1.0	8	68	284
fruit & yogurt, dried, 100 g	3.8	1.9	77	386	1637
mixed fruit, jar, 100 g	0.2	1.4	15	64	270
pasta bolognese, jar, 100 g	1.6	0.5	9	65	274
porridge, creamed, jar, 100 g	2.5	0.4	12	80	338
rice, baby, dried, 100 g	1.7	2.0	86	391	1658
rice pudding, jar, 100 g	3.3	0.1	13	92	387
roast pork & apple, dried, 100 g	10	2.2	66	404	1687
rusk, 1, 17 g	1.2	0.4	13	69	290
rusk, reduced sugar, 1, 17 g	1.5	0.5	13	70	293
seasonal vegetable & chicken, dried, reconstituted, 100 g	1.4	1	17	93	391
strawberry cheesecake, jar, 100 g	2.8	0.3	12	81	342
vegetables, beans & bacon, jar, 100 g	3	1.6	7	69	290
vegetables, cheese & pasta, organic, jar, 100 g	2.2	0.9	10	71	299
vegetables, pasta & pork, jar, 100 g	2.7	1.5	7	65	270
BACON					
gammon rasher, grilled, 170 g	21	0	0	388	1620
rasher, back, grilled, 1, 25 g	8	0	0	101	420
rasher, back, microwaved, 1, 25 g	6	0	0	77	319
rasher, middle, grilled, 1, 40 g	14	0	0	166	689
rasher, streaky, grilled, 1, 20 g	7	0	0	84	350
BAMBOO SHOOTS					
canned, drained, 140 g	0.3	++	1	15	63

B

BEANS

Beans contain varying amounts of protein, carbohydrate, vitamins and minerals (see page 96). They are an excellent source of fibre, especially soluble fibre, which helps to lower blood cholesterol levels. They are also low in fat.

Cooking dried beans

Dried beans, such as red kidney beans, contain natural toxins that need to be de-activated before use. Make sure that dried beans are soaked for 6–8 hours or overnight, drained and boiled hard in fresh water for at least 10 minutes before cooking.

Protein providers

Beans are a useful source of protein, especially for vegetarians. This protein is enhanced if the beans are eaten with a starchy non-meat protein, such as bread or rice (e.g. baked beans on toast, or chilli beans and rice).

FOOD	FAT g	FIBRE g	CARB g	ENERGY kcal	kJ
BANANAS					
green, raw, peeled, 100 g	++	2.2	22	89	379
plantain, boiled, 200 g	0.4	4.4	57	224	954
plantain, raw, 100 g	0.3	2.3	29	117	500
raw, peeled, 100 g	0.3	3.1	23	95	403
BEANS					
adzuki, dried, boiled, 120 g	0.2	++	27	148	630
baked, in tomato sauce, 100 g	0.6	6.9	15	84	355
baked, in tomato sauce, reduced sugar, 100 g	0.4	3.7	13	75	320
beansprouts, mung, raw, 1 tbsp, 20 g	0.1	1.1	1	6	26
black-eyed, dried, boiled, 100 g	0.7	++	20	116	494
broad, boiled, 100 g	0.6	++	12	81	344
butter, canned, drained, 100 g	0.5	++	13	77	327
green/French, raw, 100 g	0.5	3	3	24	99
red kidney, canned, 100 g	0.6	8.5	18	100	424
runner, boiled, 90 g	0.4	2.8	2	16	68
soya, dried, boiled, 100 g	7	++	5	141	590
BEEF					
corned, canned, 1 slice, 38 g	5	0	0	82	344
fillet steak, lean, grilled, 120 g	10	0	0	226	949
flank, lean, pot-roasted, 2 slices, 90 g	13	0	0	228	953
minced, extra lean, casseroled, 100 g	7	0.2	3	121	504
pastrami, 100g	1	1	0.1	95	402
rump steak, lean, grilled, 150 g	9	0	0	252	1062
sirloin steak, grilled, 180 g	23	0	0	383	1598
stewing steak, lean, 100 g	6	0	0	185	777
topside, lean, roast, 90 g	4	0	0	140	593
BEETROOT					
boiled, peeled, 1, 35 g	0	0.8	3	16	68
pickled, 5 slices, 50 g	0	1.3	3	14	59
BEVERAGES/HOT					
cappuccino coffee, retail, 450 ml					
full-fat milk	9	0	15	180	752
semi-skimmed milk	5	0	15	140	585
skimmed milk	0	0	15	110	46
chocolate, instant, low calorie, sachet, 28g	0.9	++	4	35	140
chocolate, instant, regular, sachet, 28 g	4	++	18	120	505

B

BEVERAGES

Coffee, tea and hot chocolate are popular beverages and can be beneficial if drunk in moderation. Cold beverages like fruit juices, fruit drinks and carbonated soft drinks are also favourite beverages, especially among children (see page 87).

Nutritional content

Cocoa and hot chocolate contain a trace of fibre, but tea and coffee have none as well as a minimal vitamin content. Coffee, cocoa and tea (especially green tea) contain amounts of antioxidants which may help reduce the risk of heart disease and some cancers.

Caffeine

Caffeine acts as a stimulant and can be addictive. A small amount is a good 'wake-up', but too much causes rapid heart action and may be harmful. It is healthiest to limit daily intake of coffee and tea to 2–3 cups.

Low or no caffeine

Reduce your caffeine intake by switching to naturally caffeine-free herbal or fruit teas or substituting decaffeinated coffee and tea. Always check food labels for caffeine content – some is lost in the roasting process, so high-roast coffee beans are lower in caffeine than medium-roast.

Cordials

Cordials, fruit squashes and carbonated drinks may contain additives, some natural and some artificial. Lower sugar or diet alternatives have artificial sweeteners that reduce their calorie values.

FOOD	FAT g	FIBRE g	CARB g	ENERGY kcal	ENERGY kJ
(BEVERAGES/HOT)					
cocoa, full-fat milk, 1 tsp sugar, 200 ml	8	0.4	14	152	640
cocoa, semi-skimmed milk, 1 tsp sugar, 200 ml	4	0.2	14	114	486
coffee, full-fat milk, 225 ml	0.9	0	1	16	70
coffee, semi-skimmed milk, 225 ml	0.5	0	2	16	65
coffee, skimmed milk, 225 ml	0	0	2	11	46
latte coffee, retail, 450 ml					
full-fat milk	14	0	22	270	1129
semi-skimmed milk	7	0	22	220	920
skimmed milk	1	0	22	160	669
iced coffee latte, retail, 450 ml					
full-fat milk	8	0	13	160	669
semi-skimmed milk	5	0	14	130	543
skimmed milk	0	0	14	100	418
latte tea, retail, full-fat milk, 450 ml	5	0	52	320	1338
malted milk, powder, 1 cup, 20 g	1	0.8	15	76	322
malted milk, powder, low-fat, 20 g	1.2	0.6	13	72	303
mocha coffee, retail, large, 450 ml					
full-fat milk	21	2	40	370	1547
semi-skimmed milk	16	2	40	340	1421
skimmed milk	11	2	40	290	1212
tea, black, 250 ml	0	0	0	0	0
tea, full-fat milk, 250 ml	1.0	0	1	20	80
tea, herbal, infusion, 250 ml	0	0	0.5	3	33
tea, semi-skimmed milk, 250 ml	0.5	0	2	18	70
tea, skimmed milk, 250 ml	0	0	2	14	59
BISCUITS					
chocolate chip, 1 small, 8 g	2	0.1	5	39	163
chocolate, full-coated, 1, 25 g	7	0.7	17	131	549
crackers, low-fat, 2, 10 g	0.1	++	8	36	152
cream crackers, 2, 14 g	2	0.9	10	62	260
digestive, chocolate, 1, 17 g	4	0.5	11	84	352
digestive, plain, 1, 13 g	3	0.6	9	61	257
fruit shortcake, 1, 8 g	1.6	0.2	6	38	161
gingernuts, 1 small, 10 g	1.5	0.2	8	46	192
oatmeal, 1, 14 g	3	0.7	9	69	289
sandwich, 1, 10 g	3	0.1	7	51	215

B

BREAD

Bread is a useful source of energy, protein, fibre, vitamins and minerals (see page 96). Five slices of ordinary sliced bread a day provides about one-fifth of your daily fibre and protein requirements. Bread itself is not particularly fattening – it's what we add to it that makes up the calories.

Wholemeal & Granary

Wholemeal and Granary breads are milled from the whole grain and are naturally higher in fibre and some minerals and vitamins than white bread. However, white bread is now often fortified with calcium, iron and B vitamins.

Fat and salt

Most breads are fairly low in fat, but croissants, brioche, cholla, focaccia and olive ciabatta may contain butter, eggs or olive oil. All bread has a fairly high salt content – eating a lot of it may take you beyond the recommended daily salt intake.

For those who suffer from allergies, there are now some breads that are gluten, wheat or yeast free.

FOOD	FAT g	FIBRE g	CARB g	ENERGY kcal	kJ
(BISCUITS)					
semi-sweet (rich tea, petit-beurre), 1, 15 g	2.5	0.3	11	69	289
water, 2, 14 g	1.8	0.9	11	62	260
BLACKBERRIES					
cooked with sugar, 100 g	0.2	5	14	56	239
cooked without sugar, 100 g	0.2	6	4	21	88
cooked with sugar, and apple, 100 g	0.1	3.6	18	70	300
raw, 100 g	0.2	6.6	5	25	104
BLACKCURRANTS					
canned in juice, 140 g	0	6	11	43	189
canned in syrup, 140 g	0	5	26	101	428
raw, 100 g	0	7.8	7	28	121
cooked with sugar, 140 g	0	9	21	81	353
BLUEBERRIES					
raw,100 g	0.2	2.5	7	30	128
BRAN (see Cereals)					
BREAD					
bagel, plain, 1	1.4	3.1	42	216	916
bagel, sweet, 1	2	2.3	44	266	1129
breadsticks, 1	0.6	++	5	27	116
brown bread, 1 large slice, 38 g	0.8	2.2	17	83	352
brown roll, crusty, 1, 48 g	1.3	3.4	24	122	521
brown roll, soft, 1, 48 g	1.8	3.1	25	129	547
chapati, made with fat, 1, 60 g	7.8	4.2	29	197	830
chapati, made without fat, 1, 55 g	0.6	3.5	24	111	473
ciabatta, 100 g	5	4.2	52	280	1184
croissant, 1, 60 g	12	1.5	23	216	903
crumpet, toasted, 1, 40 g	0.4	1.2	17	80	338
currant loaf, 1 small slice, 25 g	1.9	0.9	13	72	305
focaccia, 50 g	5	1.1	23	145	610
French, half baguette, 120 g	3	6.1	67	324	1379
gluten-free rice, 1 slice, 38 g	3	2.0	14	86	360
Granary, 1 large slice, 38 g	1	2.5	18	89	380
hamburger bun, 1, 85 g	4	3.4	42	224	953
muffin, English, 1	1	1.8	27	144	611
malt, 1 small slice, 35 g	0.8	2.3	20	94	399
milk, 1 small slice, 35 g	3	0.9	17	104	437

B

BUTTER

Butter is obtained by skimming milk, then churning the cream until the fat separates from the liquid buttermilk. The result is almost pure fat, with only a small amount of water and a trace of the solid part of the milk remaining.

Nutritional content

Butter contains more than 80 per cent fat, most of which is saturated. It contains varying amounts of the fat-soluble vitamins A, D and E and also some carotene. The protein, calcium and other minerals and vitamins from the milk are lost with the removal of the buttermilk. Salt has been traditionally added as a preservative, but low-salt and salt-free butters are also made and keep well in the fridge.

Alternatives to butter

Margarine, processed with vegetable oils and water, has a similar fat content to butter. Hard (solid) margarine contains saturated fat but soft and polyunsaturated varieties are also made. Low-fat spreads are manufactured using the same hydrogenation process as margarine, but using a much higher water content. For anyone keeping to a low-fat diet, spreads with a fat content of 5 per cent are available.

Nutritional content of butter alternatives

In the UK, vitamins A and D must be added to margarine, making them a better source of these vitamins than butter. Many low-fat spreads also contain added vitamins.

B

FOOD	FAT g	FIBRE g	CARB g	ENERGY kcal	kJ
(BREAD)					
naan, 160g	20	3.5	80	538	2264
pitta, white, 1, 60 g	0.8	2.1	29	147	624
pitta, wholemeal, 1, 60 g	0.9	3.1	27	146	618
poppadums, fried, 1, 13 g	2	1.2	5	48	201
rye, 1 small slice, 25 g	0.4	1.5	11	55	233
soda, 1 large slice, 38 g	0.9	0.9	21	98	416
tortilla, wheat flour, 1, 30 g	0.3	0.8	18	79	334
white, 1 large slice, 35 g	0.7	1.3	17	82	351
white, reduced starch, 1 large slice, 20 g	0.4	0.6	9	46	197
wholemeal, 1 large slice, 38 g	0.9	2.8	16	82	347
wholemeal, reduced starch, 1 large slice, 20 g	0.6	1.4	7	43	183
wholemeal roll, 1, 48 g	1.4	4.2	23	116	492
BROCCOLI					
green, boiled, 100 g	0.8	++	1	24	100
green, raw, 100 g	0.9	++	2	33	138
BRUSSELS SPROUTS					
raw, 100 g	1.4	3.8	4	42	177
boiled, 100 g	1.3	2.6	4	35	153
BUCKWHEAT KERNELS					
boiled, 100 g	2.5	2.1	73	334	1400
BULGAR					
(cracked wheat) cooked, 100 g	2.5	++	69	319	1340
BUTTER					
10 g	8	0	0	74	303
ghee, av. portion, 10 g	10	0	0	90	369
spreadable, 10 g	8.3	0	0	75	306
CABBAGE					
Chinese, raw, 40 g	0.1	++	1	5	20
green, boiled, 100 g	0.5	2.6	2	17	372
green, raw, 100 g	0.4	2.9	4	26	109
red, boiled, 60 g	0.2	1.5	1.4	9	37
red, raw, 100 g	0.3	3.1	4	21	89
white, raw, 100 g	0.2	2.4	5	21	113
CAKES/PASTRIES/BUNS					
Bakewell tart, iced individual, 1	8	0.6	27	190	796
Battenburg, 1 slice, 32 g	6	0.5	16	118	496

C

CAKES

Cakes come in all shapes and sizes – some may be very high in fat and sugar while others have a relatively low-fat, high-fibre content. The secret of a good diet is not so much what you eat, but how often you eat it. Enjoy a piece of cake as a treat now and then.

Low-fat choices

Remember there are no 'bad' foods, only bad diets. If you find it difficult to resist cakes but want to improve your diet, experiment with low-fat recipes or choose low-fat cakes when you shop. Aim for healthy ingredients, too, such as fruit or wholemeal flour. Try low-fat date loaf (high in sugar and fibre but low in fat), wholemeal hot-cross buns or fruit-filled teacakes.

Nutritional content

While the majority of cakes are concentrated sources of fat and sugar, some varieties provide a good source of nutrition. A traditional fruit cake is packed with dried fruit, is high in fibre and contains some minerals and vitamins such as vitamins A and D.

C

FOOD	FAT g	FIBRE g	CARB g	ENERGY kcal	kJ
(CAKES/PASTRIES/BUNS)					
bran loaf, 1 slice, 30 g	0.5	1.6	18	76	324
carrot cake, soft cheese topping, 100 g	15	0.9	49	343	1440
cheesecake, American-style, individual, 100 g	21	0.9	36	347	1449
cheesecake, frozen, 100 g	11	0.9	33	241	1013
Chelsea bun, 1, 78 g	11	1.7	44	285	1203
chocolate, sponge, 1 slice, 60 g	16	2.3	30	274	1145
chocolate marshmallow teacake, 1, 18 g	3	0.2	12	75	320
chocolate, with butter icing, 1 slice, 100 g	30	3	51	481	2009
crispie cake (chocolate & cereal), 1, 25 g	5	0.2	18	116	488
currant bun/ teacake, 1, 60 g	5	1.1	32	176	750
Danish pastry, 1, 110 g	19	3.0	56	411	1728
éclair, cream-filled, frozen, 1, 35 g	11	0.5	9	139	576
fruitcake, plain, 1 slice, 60 g	8	1.5	35	212	894
fruitcake, rich, 1 slice, 70 g	8	2.2	42	239	1007
gâteau, 1 slice, 85 g	14	0.4	37	286	1201
gingerbread, 1 slice, 50 g	6	0.7	32	190	799
Greek pastry (baklava), 100 g	17	1.9	40	322	1349
hot cross bun, 1, 50 g	3	1.1	29	155	657
iced fancy, 1, 30 g	5	0.7	21	122	515
jam tart, 1, 34 g	4	0.9	22	125	525
Madeira, 1 slice, 40 g	7	0.5	23	157	661
muffin, blueberry, 1, 85 g	14	1.5	37	277	1158
muffin, chocolate chip, 1, 85 g	13	0.8	38	280	1170
sponge, butter icing, 1 slice, 60 g	18	0.4	31	294	1228
sponge, fatless, 1 slice, 58 g	4	0.6	31	171	1152
sponge, jam-filled, 1 slice, 60 g	3	0.7	39	181	768
Swiss roll, chocolate individual, 1, 25 g	3	0.6	15	84	355
vanilla slice, individual, 1, 60 g	11	0.5	24	198	830
Welsh cake, 1, 30 g	6	0.5	19	129	542
CAROB					
powder, 40 g	0	++	15	64	272
CARROT					
canned, 100g	0.3	++	4	20	87
juice, 125 ml	0.1	++	7	30	129
old, boiled, 70 g	0.3	2.0	3	17	70
young, raw, 50 g	0.3	1.3	3	15	63

C

CEREAL, BREAKFAST

Breakfast cereals are a good way to start the day or to eat as a snack, perhaps before bed. The range of cereals available is enormous – choose varieties that you and your family enjoy eating, but do check out the nutritional value.

A balanced breakfast

All breakfast cereals contain some fibre, but wholegrain varieties have greater amounts. A bowl of wholegrain cereal with skimmed or semi-skimmed milk, plus a piece of fruit or glass of fruit juice provides a well-balanced breakfast.

Added nutrition

Many cereals are fortified with vitamins such as the important B vitamins and minerals such as iron. Some cereals are also fortified with vitamin D, which can be a useful source in the winter months when it's natural source (sunlight) is lacking.

Added sugar and salt

Choose cereals with little or no added sugar or salt. To sweeten your cereals, choose natural sweeteners such as fruit or yogurt.

C

FOOD	FAT g	FIBRE g	CARB g	ENERGY kcal	ENERGY kJ
CASSAVA					
boiled, 100 g	0.2	1.5	34	130	552
raw, 100 g	0.2	1.7	37	142	607
CAULIFLOWER					
baked with cheese, 200 g	14	2.8	10	210	876
boiled, 100 g	0.9	1.6	2	28	117
raw, 50 g	0.4	0.9	2	17	71
CELERIAC					
boiled, 120 g	0.6	5.3	2	18	74
raw, 120 g	0.5	6.1	3	22	88
CELERY					
boiled, 50 g	0.2	1.0	0.4	4	17
raw, 1 stick, 30 g	0.1	0.5	0.3	2	10
CEREALS/BARS					
apple & blackberry with yogurt, 29 g	3.2	++	21	121	510
fruit & fibre, 28 g	2.5	1.0	18	96	404
fruit & nut, with milk chocolate, 29 g	4.2	++	20	125	525
hazelnut, organic, 33 g	7.2	2.6	19	151	634
strawberry, with cereal mix, 37 g	3.5	1.0	26	140	550
CEREALS/BREAKFAST					
whole bran 30 g	1	9.0	14	78	333
bran, natural wheat, 1 tsp, 7 g	0.4	2.8	2	14	61
bran strands, 30 g	0.9	8.5	16	82	349
bran flakes, 30 g	0.6	5.2	21	95	406
bran flakes, oat, 30 g	1.2	++	22	107	456
chocolate flavoured rice pops, 30 g	0.3	0.3	28	115	491
corn flakes, 30 g	0.2	1.0	26	107	455
corn flakes with nuts, 30 g	1.0	0.5	27	119	507
fruit & fibre flakes, 30 g	1.4	3.0	22	106	449
grapenuts, 30 g	0.2	1.9	24	104	443
muesli, 100 g	7	8	66	365	1542
muesli, crunchy, 100 g	13	5.0	66	410	1727
porridge, with water, 160 g	2	1.3	14	78	334
porridge, with milk, 160 g	8.1	1.3	22	93	400
puffed wheat, 20 g portion	0.3	1.8	14	64	273
puffed rice, 30 g	0.2	0.3	29	115	490
quick-cook oatmeal, with milk, 180 g	14	12.2	125	700	2961

C

CHEESE

Cheese is made and eaten in nearly every country in the world. Most is made from cow's milk, but goat and sheep cheeses are also widely available. Soya beans are used to produce a milk-free option.

Nutritional content

Cheese retains most of the protein, fat, vitamin A and calcium from the milk used to make it. Full-fat milk cheese has a high-fat content and no carbohydrate. Fibre is only present if seeds or nuts are added.

A hard cheese like Edam has a slightly lower fat content. Lower fat Cheddar-type cheeses are also made. However, salt is an important added ingredient to hard cheeses. Softer cheeses like Brie are lower in fat and soft, unripened cottage cheese or fromage frais may be very low-fat, whereas cream cheese can be very high-fat. Soft cheeses are also lower in salt than hard. However, pregnant women and the elderly are advised to avoid all unpasteurized soft cheeses.

Alternative cheeses

Alternative cheeses made with non-animal rennet are available for vegetarians. People who are sensitive to cow's milk can enjoy cheeses made from the milk of other animals, such as goats and sheep.

C

FOOD	FAT g	FIBRE g	CARB g	ENERGY kcal	kJ
(CEREALS/BREAKFAST)					
rice-based crispies, 30 g	0.3	0.3	27	111	472
shredded wheat biscuits, 2, 44 g	1.0	4.4	30	143	609
sugar-coated puffed rice, 30 g	0.3	1.4	25	97	414
sultana bran flakes, 50 g	0.8	7.8	34	151	644
waffles, pre-cooked with jam, 1, 50 g	5	0.7	35	195	825
wholewheat biscuits, large, 40 g	0.8	4.6	30	137	582
wholewheat biscuits, small, 45 g	0.7	4.9	33	149	635
CHARD					
Swiss, boiled, 100 g	0.1	++	3	20	84
Swiss, raw, 100 g	0.2	++	3	19	81
CHEESE					
Brie, 40 g	11	0	0	128	529
Camembert, 40 g	10	0	0	119	493
Cheddar type, 40 g	14	0	0	165	683
cottage, plain reduced fat, carton 112 g	1.6	0	4	87	371
cottage, with extras, carton, 112 g	4.3	++	3	106	448
cream, full-fat, 30 g	14	0	0	132	542
Danish blue, 30 g	9	0	0	104	431
double Gloucester, 30 g	10	0	0	122	503
Edam, 40 g	10	0	0	133	553
Edam-type, reduced fat, 40 g	4	0	0	92	383
Emmenthal, 40 g	12	0	0	153	635
feta, 40 g	8	0	0	98	407
goat, soft, 30 g	5	0	0.3	59	247
Gouda, 40 g	12	0	0	150	622
Gruyère, 40 g	13	0	0	164	678
halloumi, 40 g	9	0	0.6	116	486
Jarlsberg, 40 g	11	0	0	144	600
Lancashire, 40 g	12	0	0	149	665
Leicester, 40 g	14	0	0	160	665
mozzarella, 30 g	6	0	0	87	361
Parmesan 30 g	10	0	0	136	564
processed, plain, 1 slice, 20 g	5	0	0.2	66	273
quark, 30 g	0+	0	1.2	22	94
ricotta, 30 g	3	0	0.6	43	180
Roquefort, 40 g	13	0	0	150	621

CHICKEN

This inexpensive meat is easily available: fresh, frozen or chilled, in portions or whole. Choose from standard chickens to corn-fed, free-range and organic. An excellent source of low-fat protein, chicken can be prepared and cooked in a multitude of ways.

Fat

Most of the fat in chicken is contained in the skin. Without skin, the chicken flesh is very low in fat, delicate in flavour and adapts to many different recipes. Light (breast) meat is lower in fat than dark (leg and thigh) meat. Some of the fat in the chicken skin is lost during cooking – pour the fat off roast chicken, grill portions on a rack so that the fat drains away.

Grilling

To grill skinless chicken, try lining the grill with non-stick kitchen foil and baste the meat with lemon juice instead of oil.

Takeaway chicken

Breaded and deep-fried or spit-roasted and basted with lots of oil, either way these should be an occasional treat as they are high in fat.

HEALTH WARNING

Chicken can carry the salmonella bacteria, so must be stored and cooked properly. Frozen chicken should be completely thawed before cooking and all chicken should be cooked thoroughly before serving.

C

FOOD	FAT g	FIBRE g	CARB g	ENERGY kcal	ENERGY kJ
(CHEESE)					
soft, full-fat, 30 g	9	0	0	94	388
soya, 40 g	11	0	0+	128	528
spread, low-fat, with chives, 100 g	16	0.3	3	185	760
spread, very low-fat, plain, 100 g	6	0	4	128	537
Stilton, blue, 35 g	12	0	0	144	595
Wensleydale, 40 g	13	0	0	151	625
vegetarian, Cheddar-type, 100 g	36	0	0	425	1759
CHERRIES					
canned in syrup, 100 g	0	0.7	19	71	305
glacé, 6, 30 g	0	0.4	20	75	321
raw, 100 g (weight with stones)	0.1	1.2	10	39	168
CHICKEN					
breast, grilled, with skin 100 g	6	0	0	173	728
breast, grilled, without skin 100 g	3	0	0	148	626
breast strips, stir-fried, 100 g	5	0	0	161	677
dark meat, roasted, 100 g	11	0	0	196	820
drumstick, casseroled, with skin, 90 g (with bone)	8	0	0	127	528
drumstick, casseroled, meat only, 50 g	5	0	0	93	386
light meat, roasted, 100 g	4	0	0	154	646
portion, fried, meat, skin & bone, 1, 70 g	8	0	0	125	677
quarter, roast, without skin, 190 g (with bone)	5	0	0	140	590
CHICKPEAS					
canned, 100 g	3	++	16	115	487
CHICORY					
boiled, 100 g	0.3	++	2	7	31
raw, 100 g	0.6	++	3	11	45
CHILLI					
green, raw, 1, 20 g	0.1	++	0.1	4	17
powder, 1 tsp, 3 g	0.8	0+	0+	0+	0+
red, raw, 1, 20 g	0.3	++	2	23	97
CHINESE CABBAGE (see Cabbage)					
CHIVES					
fresh, 2 tbsp, 40 g	0.2	++	0.7	9	39
CHOCOLATE					
buttons, 33 g	10	0	19	173	724
coated biscuit fingers, 4-finger bar, 48 g	13	++	29	247	1032

C

CHOCOLATE

First consumed as a fairly bitter-tasting hot drink, chocolate has developed into confectionery, an ingredient in cakes and desserts and an addiction for many of us!

sugar, with white chocolate the highest. Cocoa powder has no added sugar, but some drinking chocolate powders include a high sugar content. There is some iron in chocolate – it is highest in dark chocolate and cocoa and lowest in white.

HEALTH WARNING

Chocolate can trigger migraine in some sufferers. It also has mildly stimulative and addictive properties.

Nutritional content

All types of chocolate are high in fat, which is mostly saturated. There is a very small amount of starch in chocolate as well as fibre. Adding nuts to chocolate increases the fibre value.

Dark, milk and white chocolate have varying amounts of added

FOOD	FAT g	FIBRE g	CARB g	ENERGY kcal	kJ
(CHOCOLATE)					
coated caramel bar, 1, 50 g	11	++	32	240	1005
coated coconut bar, 1, 57 g	15	++	32	268	1122
coated malt balls, 37 g	9	++	23	177	740
coated nougat & toffee bar, 54 g	9	++	37	243	1020
dark, 100 g	26	++	61	500	2080
fruit & nut, dark, 100 g	28	6.4	55	494	2066
fruit & nut, milk, 100 g	26	++	56	490	2060
flake, 1 stick, 32 g	10	0	19	180	755
in crisp sugar shells, 1 tube, 37 g	7	0.3	31	195	820
milk, 7-square bar, 49 g	15	0	28	260	1065
powder, drinking, 18 g	1	0+	14	66	280
spread, chocolate nut, 8 g	3	0.1	5	44	184
white, 1 square, 7 g	2	0	4	37	155
milk, 49 g bar, 7 squares	15	0	28	260	1065
milk, 49 g bar, 7 squares	15	0	28	260	1065
CHUTNEY, PICKLES & RELISHES					
brinjal (aubergine) pickle, 30 g	7	0.3	10	110	458
mango chutney, oily, 20 g	2	0.3	10	57	240
mango chutney, sweet, 20 g	0	++	10	38	161
tomato chutney, 20 g	0	++	6	26	108
vegetable pickle, sweet, 30 g	0.1	0.4	10	42	182
CLEMENTINES (see Mandarin Oranges)					
COCOA,					
powder, 1 heaped tsp, 6 g	1.3	++	0.7	19	79
CORDIALS (see Soft Drinks)					
CORN					
baby, canned, 100 g	0.4	++	2	23	96
cob, whole, boiled, 100 g	1.4	2.5	12	66	280
corn, baby, raw, 100 g	0.4	2.2	7	30	130
kernels, canned, 30 g	0.4	1.2	8	37	156
COURGETTE					
boiled, 90 g	0.4	++	2	17	73
raw, 1, 90 g	0.4	++	4	23	95
COUSCOUS					
cooked, 100 g	0.4	0+	24	107	449

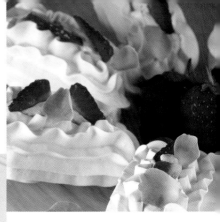

C

CREAM

Cream is made from fresh milk by skimming off the fatty layer that rises to the surface. It has a high-fat content, so should be consumed sparingly.

Fat content

The fat content of the types of cream available differs enormously:

half cream	12 % by weight as milk fat
single cream	19 %
whipping cream	35 %
double cream	48 %
clotted cream	55 %

Lower fat choices

Soured cream and crème fraîche are made by adding a bacterial culture to cream to thicken and slightly sour it. The fat content depends on the original cream used but low-fat varieties are widely available. Low-fat, thick crème fraîche can be used as a delicious alternative to cream sweet and savoury dishes.

Nutritional content

Cream is well known for being a high-fat, high-calorie food. The number of calories depends on the amount of fat that is present. All types of cream contain some vitamin A and D. Lower fat varieties also contain B vitamins.

C

FOOD	FAT g	FIBRE g	CARB g	ENERGY kcal	kJ
CRANBERRY					
raw, 100 g	0.1	3.8	3	15	65
juice, 250 ml	0	0	29	123	518
sauce, 25 g	0	++	10	38	162
CREAM					
(buttermilk & oil), full fat, 100g	36	0.3	4	349	1435
(buttermilk & oil), single, 100g	10	0.3	6	124	513
clotted, 100 g	64	0	2	586	2413
crème fraîche, 100g	40	0	3	380	1567
double, 100 g	48	0	3	449	1849
half, 100 g	13	0	4	148	613
single, 100 g	19	0	4	198	817
soured, 100 g	20	0	4	205	845
UHT spray can, 10 g	3	0	0.3	31	127
whipping, 100 g	39	0	3	373	1539
CRISPBREAD					
crackerbread, 1 slice, 5 g	0.2	0.2	4	19	81
crisp rounds, 1, 7 g	0.3	0.3	6	31	130
multigrain, 1 slice, 11 g	0.7	1.9	6	37	155
rye, 1 slice, 9 g	0.1	1.5	6	28	120
sesame seed, 1 slice, 9 g	0.6	1.5	5	30	128
toasts, 1, 10 g	0.8	0.4	7	41	170
CROISSANT					
plain, 1, 60 g	12	1.5	23	216	903
chocolate-filled, 1, 60 g	14	1.9	25	240	1006
CRUMPET					
1, toasted, 40 g	0.4	1.2	17	80	338
CUCUMBER					
raw, 5 slices, 30 g	0	0.2	0.4	3	12
CURRANTS (see Dried Fruit)					
CURRY PASTE					
ready-made, 25 g	5	++	2	59	244
powder, 1 tsp, 3g	0.3	++	1	7	29
CUSTARD					
egg, baked, 100 g	6	0	11	118	494
powder, with full-fat milk, 100 g	5	0	17	117	495
powder, with semi-skimmed milk, 100 g	2	0	17	94	403
ready-made, 100 g	3	0	16	100	420

D

DESSERTS

If you enjoy eating sweet foods you may find it hard to resist the tempting array of desserts that are now available, either on the dessert trolley or on the supermarket shelves. Be aware that some desserts are not only high in sugar, but also in fat – pastries with cream, chocolate puddings, etc. Any of these desserts are fine for an occasional treat, but not every day.

Low-fat desserts

Check labels when shopping and choose low-fat desserts wherever possible. Fruit is always a good choice – try a tropical fruit salad, or baked apples stuffed with dried fruit, or pears baked in red wine.

Instead of an elaborate ice cream, have a sorbet – high in sugar but fat-free. A meringue shell (without cream) contains sugar but no fat.

Serve desserts with low-fat fromage frais or yogurt.

D

FOOD	FAT g	FIBRE g	CARB g	ENERGY kcal	kJ
CUSTARD APPLE					
bullock's heart, raw, 100 g	0.4	++	16	70	298
sugar apple, raw, 100 g	0.3	++	16	69	296
DAMSONS (see Plums)					
DATES					
dried, 100 g	0.2	7.8	68	270	1151
dried, 100 g (weight with stones)	0.2	6.5	57	227	969
fresh, 100 g (weighed with stones)	0.1	3.1	27	107	456
DESSERTS & PUDDINGS					
apple pie, 100 g	13	2.1	36	266	1115
apple pie, wholemeal pastry, 100 g	14	3.5	32	257	1079
apple sponge, 150 g	20	2.6	43	362	1514
banana split, with ice cream, 200 g	22	2.8	39	364	1522
banoffee cream pie, 70 g	15	2.7	24	239	1500
blackcurrant pie, retail, 110 g	15	5.3	38	288	1209
bread pudding, 190 g	18	5.7	94	564	2379
chocolate mousse, 100 g	5	0	20	139	586
chocolate mousse, rich, 100 g	7	0	26	178	751
chocolate pudding with sauce, canned, 78 g	7	1.1	38	227	954
Christmas pudding, retail, 100 g	12	3.4	56	329	1388
crème caramel, 90 g	2	0	19	98	416
crumble, apple, 100 g	7	2.1	37	207	1388
crumble, fruit, 170 g	12	3.7	58	337	1420
crumble, fruit, wholemeal, 170 g	12	5.1	54	328	1382
frozen mousse, fruit, 100 g	7	0.3	21	157	658
fruit pie, individual, 110 g	15	2.4	37	286	1198
ice-cream sponge roll, 50 g	3	0.4	17	100	424
instant dessert, with full-fat milk, 120 g	8	0.2	18	132	558
instant dessert, with skimmed milk, 120 g	4	0.2	18	100	425
jam sponge, canned, 82 g	7	0.5	42	237	999
jelly, with full-fat milk, 200 g	3	0	33	176	746
jelly, with water, 200 g	0	0	30	122	520
lemon meringue pie, 190 g	27	1.5	87	606	2550
rice/tapioca (milk) pudding, full-fat, 200 g	9	0.4	39	256	1080
rice/tapioca (milk) skimmed, 200 g	0.4	0.4	40	184	790
sponge pudding, with dried fruit, 110 g	16	1.8	53	364	1531
sponge pudding, with jam or treacle, 120 g	17	1.3	58	400	1678

D

DRESSINGS

We think of salad as a 'slimming' food, and most salad vegetables are very low in calories, avocado being a notable high-fat exception. The problem comes with the added dressing. Check the fat content on labels carefully and make low-fat dressings your first choice.

Vinaigrette salad dressing

A classical vinaigrette style salad dressing is about 3 parts oil to 1 part vinegar or lemon juice. One tablespoon of any oil (olive, corn, sunflower oil) provides 11 g fat, which is 99 calories.

RECIPES

Yogurt dressing

4 tbsp low-fat yogurt
2 tbsp lemon juice
1 tbsp chopped fresh herbs
salt and pepper

Mix the yogurt, lemon juice, herbs together in a bowl. Season to taste with salt and pepper and serve immediately.

Spicy tomato

6 tbsp tomato juice
2 tbsp vinegar
1 tbsp grated onion
2 tsp Worcestershire sauce
salt and pepper

Mix the tomato juice and vinegar together in a bowl. Add the onion, Worcestershire sauce and salt and pepper to taste and mix well.

D

FOOD	FAT g	FIBRE g	CARB g	ENERGY kcal	kJ
(DESSERTS & PUDDINGS)					
sticky toffee pudding, canned, 77 g	9	0.6	36	239	1003
tiramisù, retail, chilled, 100 g	11	++	39	286	1200
treacle tart, 100 g	14	1.4	60	368	1550
trifle, 113 g	7	0.5	25	181	762
DIPS					
cheese & chive, 100 g	22	0.1	7	245	1005
guacamole (avocado), 100 g	13	2.6	2	126	530
hummus, 30 g	4	1.0	4	56	234
mayonnaise with garlic, 100 g	50	0.1	5	480	1975
spicy tomato salsa, 100 g	1.3	0.9	8	50	205
taramasalata, 100 g	49	0.7	6	480	1980
tzatziki, 100 g	3	0.5	6	79	333
DOUGHNUTS					
jam, 1, 75 g	11	1.9	37	252	1061
ring, 1, 60 g	13	1.9	28	238	997
ring, iced, 1, 80 g	14	1.9	44	306	1288
DRESSINGS (see also Mayonnaise)					
blue cheese, 1 tbsp, 15 g	7	0	1.3	69	283
caesar (oil/vinegar/cheese), 100 g	4	0.3	4	498	2052
fat free, any, 1 tbsp, 15 g	0.2	0	2.1	10	42
Italian (oil/vinegar/lemon juice), 100 g	1	0	0.6	545	2250
low-fat, any, 1 tbsp, 15 g	0.5	0	1.4	11	45
oil & lemon, 1 tbsp, 15 g	11	0	0.4	97	399
thousand island, 1 tbsp, 15 g	4.5	++	1.9	48	200
thousand island, reduced calorie, 1 tbsp, 15 g	2.3	++	2	29	122
vinaigrette (balsamic or wine vinegar),100 g	35	0	4	333	1370
yogurt-based, 1 tbsp, 15 g	4	++	1.4	44	181
DRIED FRUIT					
currants, 25 g	0.1	1.5	17	67	285
mixed fruit, 100 g	0.4	5.6	68	268	1144
mixed peel, 25 g	0.2	++	15	58	246
raisins, 1 tbsp, 30 g	0.1	1.8	21	82	348
sultanas, 1 tbsp, 30 g	0.1	1.9	21	83	351
DUCK					
roasted, meat only, 100 g	10	0	0	189	789
roasted, with fat & skin, 100 g	38	0	0	423	1750

FAST FOOD

Most takeaway fast foods – fish and chips, chicken and chips, burger and chips, pizza – are high in fat and salt. These are fine if eaten occasionally, but not every day.

Being selective

Busy lifestyles can mean that fast foods are a necessity, but try to be selective and find foods that are lower in fat and contain a wide range of nutrients.

A hamburger (no cheese) in a bun, with lettuce and ketchup is better eaten without chips. Try a doner kebab, usually served in pitta bread with salad, or choose jacket potatoes. Potatoes are low

in fat, but resist adding butter or a mayonnaise-based filling – baked beans in a baked potato are low fat and make a good meal. A hot dog with mustard or ketchup but without onions, is another lower fat alternative.

F

FOOD	FAT g	FIBRE g	CARB g	ENERGY kcal	ENERGY kJ
EGGS					
hen, boiled or poached, 1 medium, 50 g	5	0	0	74	306
hen, fried, 1, 60 g	8	0	0	107	447
hen, scrambled with milk, 2 120 g	27	0	0.7	296	1230
hen, yolk only, raw, 18 g	6	0	0	61	252
hen, white only, raw, 32 g	0	0	0.7	12	49
duck, boiled, 1, 65 g	10	0	0	129	534
omelette, 2-egg plain, 120 g	20	0	0	229	950
quail, 1, raw, 10 g	1	0	0	15	63
ELDERBERRIES					
raw, 100 g	0.5	++	7	35	149
ENDIVE					
raw, 60 g	0	102	0.6	8	32
FALAFEL					
deep-fried, retail, 60 g	7	2.6	9	107	450
FAST FOOD/TAKEAWAY					
chicken, deep-fried, 2 pieces, 200 g	14	++	16	266	1114
chicken nuggets, deep-fried, 6	17	++	19	276	1160
chips (thick), 100 g	26	6	64	502	2102
doner kebab, lamb, with pitta/salad, 230 g	37	2.8	32	587	2450
fish (e.g. cod) in batter, deep-fried, 180 g	28	0.9	21	445	1856
frankfurter in bun, with ketchup & onions, 150 g	15	4	39	327	1371
french fries, medium, 110 g	17	3.4	37	308	1291
hamburger, 160 g	16	++	36	357	1496
hamburger, with cheese, 195 g	26	++	42	500	2105
milkshake (thick), 1, 300 g	10	0	61	374	1569
FATS & OILS (see also Margarines)					
beef dripping, 15 g	15	0	0	134	549
cocoa butter, 15 g	15	0	0	134	552
lard, 15 g	15	0	0	134	549
low-fat spread, 15 g	6	0	0	58	241
oil, any (e.g. vegetable, corn, olive), 1 tbsp, 20ml	11	0	0	99	407
suet, beef, shredded, 100 g	87	0.6	12	826	3402
suet, vegetable, 100 g	88	0	10	836	3444
very low-fat spread, 15 g	4	0	0	41	169
FENNEL					
boiled, 1, 150 g	0.3	++	2.3	17	71

FISH

Fish is very nutritious and should be encouraged on to the family menu. Today there is a wide range of fish for sale, although in parts of the world fish is a much scarcer and more expensive commodity, due to over-fishing of some seas. Fish can be roughly divided into three groups: white fish, oily or fatty fish (see page 46) and shellfish (see page 48).

White fish

White fish are saltwater fish and include cod, coley, haddock, ling, monkfish, plaice, sole, whiting and many others. These fish have a very low-fat content, although the fish liver may be high in fat. If cooked without added fat these fish are low in calories and high in protein. Cod liver oil and halibut liver oil, obtained from white fish has very high levels of vitamins A and D.

F

FOOD	FAT g	FIBRE g	CARB g	ENERGY kcal	kJ
FIGS					
dried, 100 g	1.6	12.4	53	227	967
dried, cooked with sugar, 100 g	0.8	6.5	34	143	612
raw, 1, 40 g	0.1	0.9	4	17	74
ready-to-eat, 1, 55 g	0.8	6.3	27	115	489
FISH					
anchovies, 3, 9 g	2	0	0	25	105
bass, 100 g	2.5	0	0	100	421
bloater, grilled, 100 g	17	0	0	251	1043
bream, 100 g	3	0	0	96	405
carp, raw, 100 g	4.7	0	0	112	471
clams, canned, 100 g	0.6	0	2	77	325
cod fillet, baked, 100 g	1.2	0	0	96	408
cod fillet, poached/steamed, 100 g	1	0	0	94	396
cod, deep-fried in batter, 180 g	28	0.9	21	445	1856
cod, in parsley sauce, 170 g	5	0.2	5	143	402
cod, smoked, poached, 100 g	1.6	0	0+	101	426
cod, smoked, raw, 100 g	0.6	0	0	79	333
coley, raw fillet, 100 g	1.0	0	0	82	348
coley, steamed, 100 g	1.3	0	0	105	444
conger eel, grilled, 100 g	5.5	0	0	137	478
conger eel, raw, 100 g	4.6	0	0	114	478
crabmeat, boiled, 40 g	2.2	0	0	51	214
crabmeat, canned, 85 g	0.4	0	0	65	277
crab stick, 1, 17 g	0	0	1	12	49
crayfish, raw, meat only, 100 g	0.8	0	0	67	283
cuttlefish, raw, 100 g	1	0	0	71	300
dab, raw, 100 g	1.2	0	0	74	311
Dover sole, raw, 100 g	1.8	0	0	89	374
eel, jellied, 100 g	7	0	0	98	406
eel, raw, 100 g	11	0	0	98	700
eel, smoked, 100 g	13	0	1	167	700
flounder, raw, 100 g	1.8	0	0	82	345
flounder, steamed, 100 g	2.2	0	0	101	427
flying fish, raw, 100 g	0.3	0	0	86	366
goujons, white fish, fried, 100 g	29	0.9	14	374	1553
haddock fillet, grilled, 100 g	0.8	0	0	104	442

FATTY OR OILY FISH

Oily fish includes herring, mackerel, eels, salmon, sardines, trout and many others. The higher fat content in the often pink or creamy-coloured flesh gives these fish a rich flavour. Their calorie content is higher than that of white fish, but their flavour makes a smaller portion satisfying.

Fatty acids

Oily fish, such as mackerel, sardines and pilchards are also rich in omega-3 fatty acids. These are polyunsaturated fats and can help to protect against coronary heart disease. Mackerel is a comparatively cheap fish, so it is particularly recommended as part of a healthy diet.

F

FOOD

FOOD	FAT g	FIBRE g	CARB g	ENERGY kcal	ENERGY kJ
(FISH)					
haddock fillet, in crumbs, fried, 100 g	8	0.5	10	157	657
haddock fillet, raw, 100 g	0.6	0	0	81	345
haddock, poached in milk, 100 g	4	0	0	113	47
haddock, smoked, steamed, 100 g	0.9	0	0	101	429
hake fillet, grilled, 100 g	2.7	0	0	113	310
hake, fillet, raw, 100 g	2.2	0	0	92	387
halibut, grilled, 100 g	2.2	0	0	121	345
halibut, poached in milk, 100 g	5.7	0	1	154	648
halibut, raw, 100 g	1.9	0	0	103	436
herring, canned in tomato sauce, 100 g	14	0	3	193	802
herring, dried, salted, 100 g	7	0	0	168	704
herring fillet, grilled, 100 g	11	0	0	181	756
herring fillet, raw, 1, 119 g	16	0	0	226	941
herring, pickled, 100 g	11	0	10	209	877
hilsa, raw, 100 g	19	0	0	262	1088
hoki, grilled, 100 g	2.7	0	0	121	510
hoki, raw, 100 g	1.9	0	0	85	358
jackfish, raw, 100 g	2	0	0	108	458
John Dory, raw, 100 g	1.9	0	0	89	375
kipper, boil in the bag, 100 g	17	0	0	237	984
kipper fillet, grilled, 100 g	19	0	0	255	1060
kipper, grilled, 100 g (weight with bones)	12	0	0	161	667
kipper, raw, 100 g	18	0	0	229	952
lemon sole, grilled, 100 g	1.7	0	0	97	408
lemon sole, grilled, with bones & skin, 100 g	1.1	0	0	62	261
lemon sole, steamed, 100 g	0.9	0	0	91	384
lemon sole, steamed, with bones & skin, 100 g	0.6	0	0	64	272
lemon sole, raw, 100 g	1.5	0	0	83	351
ling, raw, 100 g	0.7	0	0	82	346
lobster, meat, boiled, 85 g	1.4	0	0	88	370
lobster, whole, 500 g (weight with shell)	3	0	0	185	785
mackerel, grilled, 100 g	17	0	0	239	994
mackerel, canned in brine, drained, 100 g	18	0	0	237	985
mackerel, canned in tomato sauce, 100 g	15	0	1	206	856
mackerel, raw, 100 g	16	0	0	220	914
mackerel, smoked, 100 g	31	0	0	354	1465

F

SHELLFISH AND OTHER SEAFOOD

Shellfish includes prawns, shrimps, scampi, oysters, lobsters, scallops, cockles, mussels and many others. The total fat in shellfish is low, but all of them, particularly lobster, are high in cholesterol. Fish roe, including caviar, also has a high cholesterol level.

Cholesterol

Cholesterol is a natural constituent in the blood, and a high dietary fat intake can cause an increase in our cholesterol levels. There is some debate over the significance of cholesterol in foods, but in reality the cholesterol we take in from foods is probably much less implicated in heart disease than the fat we ingest.

It has been suggested also that the cholesterol in shellfish is of a type which does not increase human blood cholesterol. Whether or not this is true, eating shellfish in moderation is unlikely to be harmful to health.

Other nutrients

Shellfish contain small amounts of B vitamins and some varieties, especially cockles, are high in iron. They contain small amounts of other minerals, but nearly all have a high sodium chloride (salt) content.

FOOD	FAT g	FIBRE g	CARB g	ENERGY kcal	kJ
(FISH)					
monkfish, grilled, 100 g	0.6	0	0	96	314
monkfish, raw, 100 g	0.4	0	0	66	282
mullet, grey, grilled, 100 g	5.2	0	0	150	629
mullet, grey, raw, 100 g	5	0	0	150	629
mullet, red, grilled, 100 g	4.4	0	0	121	510
mullet, red, raw, 100 g	4	0	0	121	510
mussels, boiled, without shells, 40 g	1	0	0	42	176
octopus, raw, 100 g	1.3	0	0	83	352
orange roughy, raw, 100 g	7	0	0	126	527
oysters, raw, 6, 60 g	0.8	0	2	39	165
parrot fish, raw, 100 g	0.4	0	0	83	353
pilchards, canned in tomato sauce, 1, 55 g	4.5	0	0.6	79	331
plaice, in breadcrumbs, fried, 150 g	21	0.6	13	342	1427
plaice fillet, steamed, 100 g	1.5	0	0	92	389
plaice fillet, grilled, 100 g	1.7	0	0	96	404
plaice fillet, raw, 100 g	1.4	0	0	79	336
plaice, in batter, deep-fried, 200 g	34	1	24	514	2144
pollack, Alaskan, raw, 100 g	0.6	0	0	72	304
pomfret, black, raw, 100 g	2.6	0	0	99	416
pomfret, white, raw, 100 g	2.1	0	0	92	389
prawns, boiled, 60 g	0.5	0	0	59	251
red snapper fillet, fried, 100 g	3.1	0	0	126	531
red snapper, raw, 100 g	1.3	0	0	90	381
redfish, raw, 100 g	2.7	0	0	98	413
rock salmon, in batter, deep-fried, 200 g	44	1	21	590	245
rohu, raw, 100 g	1.4	0	0	79	334
salmon, canned, meat only, 100 g	7	0	0	153	644
salmon, grilled, 100 g	13	0	0	215	896
salmon, raw, 100 g	12	0	0	182	757
salmon, smoked, 56 g	2.5	0	0	80	335
salmon, steamed, 100 g	12	0	0	194	812
sardines, canned in brine, 1, 25 g	2.4	0	0	43	180
sardines, canned in oil, 1, 25 g	3.5	0	0	55	230
sardines, canned in tomato sauce, 1, 25 g	2.5	0	0.3	41	170
sardines, grilled, 100 g	10	0	0	165	815
sardines, raw, 100 g	9	0	0	165	691

F

FISH PRODUCTS

Fish products are also nutritious and can make a valuable contribution to a good diet, as well as an excellent way to serve fish to the family.

Canned fish

Canned oily fish is inexpensive and can be used for sandwiches or in home-made fish cakes. Canned sardines, pilchards, salmon and mackerel are an excellent source of vitamin D and the soft bones of salmon and sardines can be mashed into the flesh to increase the calcium content.

Fish fingers

Fish fingers are usually made from white fish, and are often very popular with children. They are not too high in fat if grilled or baked in the oven.

Fish cakes

Fish cakes, made with white or fatty fish are another way of eating fish for those who are worried about bones or the look of fish. Fish cakes can be made easily at home, using mashed potato and cooked smoked or white fish, canned tuna or salmon.

FOOD	FAT g	FIBRE g	CARB g	ENERGY kcal	kJ
(FISH)					
scallops, steamed, 100 g	1.4	0	3	118	501
scampi, in breadcrumbs, fried, 170 g	23	1.9	35	403	1685
shark, raw, 100 g	1.1	0	0	102	432
skate, fillet, grilled, 100 g	0.5	0	0	79	337
skate, in batter, fried, 200 g	20	0.4	10	336	1404
sprats, fried, meat only, 100 g	35	0	0	415	1718
squid, in batter, fried, 100 g	10	0.6	16	195	815
squid, raw, 100 g	1.7	0	1	81	344
swordfish, grilled, 100 g	5	0	0	139	583
swordfish, raw, 100 g	4	0	0	109	458
trout, brown, raw, 100 g	4	0	0	112	470
trout, rainbow, raw, 100 g	5	0	0	125	565
tuna, canned in brine, 100 g	0.6	0	0	99	422
tuna, canned in oil, 100 g	9	0	0	189	794
tuna, raw, 100 g	5	0	0	136	573
tuna, grilled, 100 g	7	0	0	166	714
turbot, grilled, 100 g	3.5	0	0	122	514
turbot, raw, 100 g	3	0	0	95	401
whitebait, in flour, deep-fried, 80 g	38	0.2	4	420	1739
whiting, raw, 100 g	0.7	0	0	81	344
whiting, steamed, 85 g	0.8	0	0	78	331
FLOUR					
arrowroot, 100 g	0.1	++	94	355	1515
buckwheat, 100 g	1.5	++	85	364	1522
carob, 100 g	0.7	++	89	180	753
chapati, brown, 100 g	1.2	10.3	74	333	1419
chapati, white, 100 g	0.5	4.1	78	335	1426
chickpea, 100 g	5	13.5	50	313	1328
cornflour, 100 g	0.7	++	92	354	1508
maize, 100 g	1	++	78	362	1515
millet, 100 g	1.7	++	75	354	1481
potato, 100 g	0.9	7	76	328	1398
rice, 100 g	0.8	++	80	366	1531
rye, whole, 100 g	2	++	76	335	1428
semolina, raw, 100 g	2	4	78	350	1489
soya, full-fat, 100 g	24	10.7	24	447	1871

F

FLOUR

Flour is made from the milling of cereals, such as wheat, maize, rice, rye and millet. In Western countries the majority of flour is produced from wheat. Flour was probably man's first convenience food and it is still valued for its versatility and many uses, such as in cakes, pasta and bread, besides its contribution to nutrition.

B vitamins thiamin and niacin are added after milling. Calcium and iron may also be added.

Wholemeal flours

The composition of wholemeal, brown and Granary flours varies. Wholemeal flour is highest in fibre and contains more minerals and vitamins than fortified white, although its calcium content may be lower.

Gluten sensitivity

The protein of wheat, rye and barley contains gluten and must be avoided by those intolerant to it. Oats contain a similar protein which does not always affect those who are sensitive.

White flour

White flour is an extraction from whole wheat resulting in the loss of certain nutrients. In some countries, including the UK, the

F

FOOD	FAT g	FIBRE g	CARB g	ENERGY kcal	kJ
(FLOUR)					
soya, low-fat, 100 g	7	13.3	28	352	1488
wheat, brown, 100 g	2	7	69	323	1377
wheat, white, breadmaking, 100 g	1.4	3.7	75	341	1451
wheat, white, plain, 100 g	1.3	3.6	78	341	1450
wheat, wholemeal, 100 g	2	8.6	64	310	1318
FRANKFURTER					
cooked, 1, 46 g	12	0	1	129	533
FROMAGE FRAIS					
fruit, small carton, 1, 60 g	4	0	8	79	331
plain, small carton, 1, 60 g	4	0	3	68	281
very low-fat, small carton, 1, 60 g	0.1	0	4	35	148
FRUIT SALAD/COCKTAIL					
canned in juice, 100 g	0	1	7	29	122
canned in syrup, 100 g	0	1	15	57	244
GARLIC					
fresh, 2 peeled cloves, 6 g	0	++	1	6	25
powder, 1 tbsp, 10 g	0	++	4	25	105
GELATINE					
powder, sachet, 15 g	0	0	0	51	215
GHERKINS					
pickled, 1 large, 36 g	0	0.4	1	5	22
GINGER					
glacé, 2 tbsp, 25 g	0.1	0.5	21	83	354
ground, 1 tbsp, 10 g	0.3	++	6	15	110
root, raw, 1 tbsp, 10 g	0.1	++	1	5	19
stem, in syrup, drained, 100 g	0.1	1.4	6.7	271	1151
GOLDEN SYRUP					
1 tbsp, 25 g	0	0	20	75	317
GOOSE					
roast, meat only, 100 g	22	0	0	319	1327
GOOSEBERRIES					
cooking, cooked with sugar, 100 g	0.3	2.3	13	54	229
cooking, cooked without sugar, 100 g	0.3	2.4	3	16	66
dessert, canned in syrup, 100 g	0.2	1.7	19	73	310
dessert, raw, 100 g	0.3	3.1	9	40	170

H

HAM

Ham is a leg of pork, which is preserved by various salting methods. Today there is a wide choice of ham available from supermarkets and delicatessens. It is a good source of protein, but buy leaner cuts of meat for a healthy diet.

Salt

Because of the salting process ham has a fairly high salt content.

Other ham

The sliced ham available in shops is sometimes formed from lean reconstituted meat. It will have a slightly higher water content, but is tasty. It is a good protein source and quite low in fat. It is excellent for sandwiches and salads.

Choice cut

The best and tastiest ham is carved from the bone, and is lean, pale pink and slightly dry looking. This is expensive, but perfect for salads and sandwiches. Try boiling or roasting your own ham joint, either boned and rolled or on the bone for a special occasion. It is delicious hot or cold.

H

FOOD	FAT g	FIBRE g	CARB g	ENERGY kcal	kJ
GRAPEFRUIT					
canned in juice, 100 g	0	0.8	7	30	120
canned in syrup, 100 g	0	0.9	16	60	257
juice, concentrate, unsweetened, 100 ml	0.5	0	41	166	709
juice, unsweetened, 100 ml	0.1	0	8	33	140
raw, I, 160 g	0.2	2.6	11	48	202
GRAPES					
raw, 100 g	0.1	0.8	15	60	257
GRAVY					
instant granules, 2 tsp, 8g	3	0	4	46	193
instant granules, mixed with water, 100 g	2	0	3	33	139
GREENGAGES					
raw, 100 g	0.1	2.3	10	41	173
raw, 100 g (weight with stones),	0.1	2.2	9	38	163
cooked, with sugar, 100 g	0.1	2.1	21	81	347
cooked, without sugar, 100 g	0.1	2.1	9	36	155
GRENADILLAS					
raw, 100 g	0.3	14	8	42	179
GUACAMOLE (see Dips)					
GUAVA					
canned in syrup, 100 g	0	3.2	16	60	258
raw, 100 g	0.5	4.7	5	26	112
HAGGIS					
boiled, 100 g	22	++	19	310	1292
HALVA					
carrot, 30 g	7	0.9	13	106	445
retail, 30 g	12	++	16	185	771
HAM					
canned, 1 slice, 35 g	2	0	0	42	176
dry-cured, breaded, 100 g	2	0	7	151	633
dry-cured prosciutto, 100g	12	0	0	220	918
ham & pork, chopped, canned, 50 g	12	0.2	0.7	138	570
honey roast, 100g	5	0	1	147	617
joint, boiled, lean, 100 g	12	0	0	204	851
joint, roasted, smoked/unsmoked, 100g	12	0	0	202	844
oak smoked, 100g	3	0	1	121	510
Parma, 50 g	6	0	0	112	466

55

K

KIWI FRUIT

Kiwi fruit, also known as Chinese gooseberries, grow on the deciduous vine Actinidia deliciosa and are now widely available. The green fruit looks very attractive sliced in a fruit salad, on a meringue pavlova or a cake, but they are also delicious simply eaten peeled.

Nutritional content

Kiwi fruit is is a very good source of vitamin C. It is not high in fibre, but contains some carotene and is high in potassium. Most children seem to enjoy its sweet taste.

SERVING SUGGESTION

For a low-fat dessert, make a meringue base as if for a pavlova. Once cooled, arrange sliced kiwi fruit over the top. Serve with low-fat fromage frais or set yogurt.

K

FOOD	FAT g	FIBRE g	CARB g	ENERGY kcal	kJ
HEART					
beef, ox, raw, 100 g	4	0	0	108	455
beef, ox, casseroled, 100 g	6	0	0	179	752
HONEY					
honeycomb, 30 g	4	0	22	84	360
strained, jar, 15 g	0	0	12	43	184
HORSERADISH					
raw, 1 tsp	0	0.4	1	3	13
sauce, retail, 15 g	1.3	++	3	23	96
HUMMUS (see Dips)					
ICE CREAM					
chocolate covered bar, 1, 50 g	12	++	12	160	666
dairy, block, vanilla, 75 g	7	0	18	146	611
dairy, block, flavoured, 75 g	6	0	19	134	563
non-dairy, reduced-calorie, 75 g	5	0	10	89	374
soft scoop, vanilla, 100 g	8	0.2	22	170	695
lolly, caramel with chocolate, 1, 75ml	14	++	26	244	1018
caramel with toffee & chocolate, 100g	12	0.3	27	222	929
soft scoop, vanilla, cherry & chocolate chip	8	0	14	133	929
cone, chocolate & hazelnut, 1, 80g	10	0.3	24	194	812
cone, vanilla & toffee	7	0.1	26	180	754
JAM					
apricot, 1 tsp, 15g	0	0.1	9	38	161
blackcurrant conserve, high fruit, 1 tsp, 15g	0.1	0.2	7	29	121
blackcurrant, reduced sugar, 1 tsp, 15g	0.1	0.1	10	40	169
fruit marmalade, 1 tsp, 8 g	0	0	6	21	89
reduced sugar, 1 tsp, 8 g	0	++	3	10	42
JELLY (see Desserts)					
KALE					
curly, boiled, 100 g	1	2.6	1	24	100
curly, raw, 100 g	2	3.3	1	33	140
KIDNEY					
beef, ox, raw, 100 g	8	0	0	86	363
lamb, raw, 100 g	3	0	0	91	385
pig, raw, 100 g	3	0	0	90	377
KIWI FRUIT					
raw, 1 medium, without peel, 60 g	0.3	++	6	29	124
raw, with peel, 60 g	0.2	++	6	25	106

L

LENTILS

Lentils, like beans, are pulses and form a major source of protein and energy in many parts of the world. The larger yellow lentils are also called split peas, and need to be soaked before cooking. Smaller lentils, such as red, green and brown need little or no soaking.

Nutritional content

Lentils are high in fibre and are a good source of non-haem (plant) iron in the vegetarian diet. They also contain useful quantities of B vitamins and zinc.

Protein

In common with other vegetable sources of protein, the protein content of lentils is improved if they are eaten with bread or rice. The amino acids of the two different proteins complement each other, so lentils eaten with naan bread provide a more useful protein than lentils or bread eaten alone.

L

FOOD	FAT g	FIBRE g	CARB g	ENERGY kcal	kJ
KOHL RABI					
boiled, 100 g	0.2	++	3	18	77
raw, 100 g	0.2	++	4	23	95
KUMQUAT					
raw, 1, 20 g	0.1	++	2	9	37
LAMB					
breast, lean, roast, 75 g	13	0	0	189	787
cutlets, best end, lean, barbecued, 100g	14	0	0	236	985
cutlets, best end, lean & fat, barbecued 100g	27	0	0	342	1420
chump chops, lean, fried in oil, 100g	11	0	0	213	892
chump chops, lean & fat, fried in oil, 100g	23	0	0	308	1278
leg, roast, lean, 150 g	12	0	0	287	1200
leg steak, lean, grilled, 9	9	0	0	198	829
loin chop, grilled, lean, 70 g	9	0	0	155	650
loin chop, grilled, lean/fat/bone, 120 g	27	0	0	332	1376
minced, casseroled, 100g	12	0	0	208	870
shoulder, roasted, lean, 75 g	8	0	0	147	614
stewing, lean & fat, casseroled, 100 g	20	0	0	279	1159
stewing, lean, casseroled, 100 g	15	0	0	240	1000
LARD (see Fats & Oils))					
LASAGNE (see Pasta/Ready Meals)					
LEEKS					
boiled, 160 g	1	3.8	4	34	139
boiled, cheese sauce, semi-skimmed milk,100 g	6	1.5	5	92	384
boiled, cheese sauce, full-fat milk, 100 g	7	1.5	5	99	412
raw, 100 g	0.5	2.8	3	22	93
LEMON					
curd, retail, 1 tsp, 15 g	0.8	0.1	9	42	177
juice, fresh, 100 ml	0	0	2	7	31
raw, with peel, no pips,100g	0.3	4.7	3	19	79
sorbet, 2 scoops, 60 g	0	0	21	79	337
LENTILS					
dahl curry, black gram, 100 g	3.4	1.9	7	74	310
green & brown, dried, boiled, 40 g	0.3	++	7	42	178
red, split, boiled, 40 g	0.2	1.3	7	40	170
yellow split peas, boiled, dried, 100g	0.9	4.6	23	126	538
yellow split peas, raw, dried, 100g	2.4	11	58	328	1396

L

LIVER

Liver is highly nutritious and makes a very tasty meal either on its own or as part of a dish. When buying, choose liver that looks bright and glossy and smells fresh. Liver is a particularly good source of iron and protein.

Nutritional content

Liver is fairly low in fat and is an excellent source of protein and iron. The vitamin A and D content is high and it is also a good source of B vitamins, particularly folate. The animal livers available are usually calf, lamb, pig or ox. Calf or lamb's liver is the most tender and delicately flavoured, while pig and ox liver are slightly firmer and stronger tasting. Chicken livers are much smaller, but equally nutritious.

Liver pâté

Many kinds of liver are used to make this delicious pâté, though it often has a very high fat content. For people who do not enjoy eating liver in its usual form, pâté is a successful alternative. It is an excellent source of iron and other vitamins and minerals.

HEALTH WARNING

Pregnant women are advised not to eat liver, because the very high vitamin A content may be harmful to the developing baby.

L

FOOD	FAT g	FIBRE g	CARB g	ENERGY kcal	kJ
LETTUCE					
cos, 100 g	0.6	1.3	2	16	65
frisee/lamb's lettuce/lollo rosso, mixed, 100g	0.2	1.6	1	13	57
iceberg, 100 g	0.3	1.3	2	13	53
raddicchio, 100 g	0.2	++	2	14	58
LIME					
juice, fresh, 100 g	0.1	0.1	2	9	36
pickle, oily, 25 g	4	1.4	2	45	185
raw, without peel, 50 g	0.2	++	0.4	5	38
LINGUINE (see Pasta)					
LIVER					
calf, fried, 40 g	5	0.1	3	102	425
chicken, fried, 40 g	4	0.1	1	78	324
lamb, fried, 100 g	14	0	4	232	970
ox, casseroled, 100 g	10	0	4	198	831
pig, casseroled, 100 g	8	0	4	189	793
LOGANBERRIES					
canned in juice, 100 g	0	3	26	101	429
cooked with sugar, 100 g	0	4.4	13	50	214
cooked without sugar, 100 g	0	4.8	3	14	62
raw, 100 g	0	5.6	3	17	73
LOQUATS					
canned in syrup, 100 g	0.1	++	22	84	351
raw, 100 g	0.2	++	6	28	351
LOTUS					
tuber, canned, 100 g	0	++	3	51	63
LYCHEES					
canned in syrup, 100 g	0	0.7	18	68	290
raw, 100 g	0.1	1.5	14	58	248
MACARONI see Pasta					
MANDARIN (LOOSE-SKINNED) ORANGES					
clementine, raw, 1, 40 g	0.1	0.7	3	15	63
mandarin segments, canned in juice, 100 g	0	0.3	8	32	135
mandarin segments, canned in syrup, 100 g	0	0.3	13	52	223
ortanique, raw, 100 g	0.2	1.8	12	49	205
satsuma, raw, peeled, 1 av., 50 g	0.1	0.9	4	18	78
tangerine, raw, peeled, 1 av., 70 g	0.1	1.2	6	25	103

M

MAYONNAISE

Mayonnaise may have been named after the French general Mahon. His chef was unable to obtain butter for hollandaise sauce, so invented this recipe, which subsequently became a classic. Mayonnaise is made from egg yolks, olive oil and a little vinegar. Good-quality mayonnaise is delicious, but is very high in fat and calories. Best quality mayonnaise should be gelatinous with a pale, shiny look.

Salads and sandwiches

Mayonnaise is a favourite addition to all kinds of salads. It is also commonly added to commercially prepared sandwiches since it improves texture, moisture and flavour. If you are counting calories, check your lunchtime salad or sandwich for mayonnaise – it will increase the fat and calorie content hugely.

Lower fat mayo

For those looking for a lower fat alternative, 'light' mayonnaise is widely available. However, despite the fact that it contains at least half the amount of fat present in the classic product, reduced-fat mayonnaise remains a fairly high-fat product.

FOOD	FAT g	FIBRE g	CARB g	ENERGY kcal	kJ
MANGETOUT					
mangetout, boiled, 100 g	0.1	4.0	3	26	111
mangetout, raw, 100 g	0.2	4.2	4	32	136
MANGO					
canned in syrup, 100 g	0	0.9	21	81	347
chutney, sweet, 1 tbsp, 25 g	0	0+	12	47	202
juice, 100 g	0.2	0+	10	39	166
raw, 150 g	0.3	4.4	21	86	368
MANGOSTEEN					
raw, 100 g	0.5	1.3	16	73	307
MAPLE SYRUP					
100 g	0	0	66	264	1122
MARGARINE (see also Fats & Oils))					
buttermilk & vegetable oil spread, 100 g	69	0	1	627	2578
dairy free, with vegetable oil, 100 g	58	1.4	0	525	2159
hard, vegetable oil, 100 g	82	0	0	740	3040
hard, vegetable oil, 11 g	9	0	0	81	334
low-fat spread, 11 g	5	0	0.1	43	177
olive oil spread, (vegetable/olive oil),100 g	59	0	1	536	2203
polyunsaturated, 11 g	9	0	0	81	334
soft, saturated, 11 g	9	0	0	81	335
MARMALADE (see Jam)					
MARROW					
boiled, 100 g	0.2	1.0	1.6	9	38
raw, 100 g	0.2	1.1	2	12	51
MARZIPAN					
home-made, 1 tbsp, 20 g	5	1.2	10	92	387
retail, 1 tbsp, 20 g	3	0.6	14	81	341
MATZOS					
square, 1 large, 22 g	0.3	0.6	18	79	334
tea, round, 1, 5 g	0.1	0.2	4	18	76
tea, wheaten, round, 1, 5 g	0.1	0.4	4	18	76
MAYONNAISE					
home-made, 30 g	26	0	0	237	974
retail, 30 g	23	0	1	207	853
retail, reduced calorie, 30 g	8	0	3	86	356

M

MILK

Milk has been valued for years as an important food, especially for children. As well as being high in protein, it is a rich source of calcium for all.

Nutritional content

Milk is the major source of calcium for children and adults alike, building and maintaining strong and healthy bones and teeth. Milk also provides useful amounts of zinc, iron and other minerals. Full-fat varieties are an excellent source of the fat-soluble vitamins A and D and all types of milk contain important levels of B vitamins. Milk is an important nutritional source for the elderly – the calcium it contains protects against osteoporosis and it is also a major source of riboflavin (vitamin B2) for many.

Other types of milk

For those who are sensitive to cow's milk, there are soya or other plant milk substitutes but select varieties fortified with calcium and other nutrients.

Fat content

Lower fat skimmed and semi-skimmed milk remain high in calcium. The percentage amount of fat in milk is approximately:

whole milk	4 %
semi-skimmed milk	2 %
skimmed milk	less than 1 %

M

FOOD	FAT g	FIBRE g	CARB g	ENERGY kcal	kJ
MEAT SUBSTITUTE					
mycoprotein, 100 g	4	++	2	86	360
mycoprotein mince, 100 g	2	6	5	94	397
MELON					
cantaloupe-type, 150 g	0.2	1.3	6	29	122
galia, 150 g	0.2	1.3	8	36	153
honeydew, 150 g	0.2	1.2	10	42	179
watermelon, 200 g	0.6	0.6	14	62	266
MERINGUE					
shell with cream, 28 g	7	0	11	105	440
shell without cream, 8 g	0	0	8	30	129
MILK					
buttermilk, 100 g	0.5	0	5	37	157
calcium-fortified, 100 g	0.5	0	6	44	186
condensed, full-fat, sweetened, 100 g	10	0	56	333	1406
condensed, skimmed, sweetened, 100 g	0.2	0	60	267	1137
dried skimmed, powder/granules, 100 g	0.6	0	53	348	1482
dried skimmed, with vegetable fat, 100 g	26	0	43	487	2038
evaporated, full-fat, 100 g	16	0	14	257	1069
flavoured, 100 g	1.5	0	11	68	287
full-fat, 100 g	4	0	5	66	275
goat, 100 g	3.5	0	4	60	253
semi-skimmed, 100 g	1.6	0	5	46	195
skimmed, 100 g	0.1	0	5	33	140
soya, flavoured, 100 g	1.7	0	4	40	168
soya, plain, 100 g	1.9	0	1	32	132
MILKSHAKE					
powder, any flavour, 15 g	<0.1	0	15	59	251
retail, 500 ml container					
banana, 100 g	0.8	0	10	61	259
raspberry, 100 g	2.1	0	11	79	333
syrup, any flavour, 20 ml	<0.1	0	6	25	108
syrup & full-fat milk, 220 ml	8	0	16	157	658
MISO					
1 heaped tbsp, 25 g	1.5	++	6	51	214
MIXED PEEL (see Dried Fruit)					

NOODLES

Noodles are available in various forms, some wheat-based noodles are similar to dried pasta, while others contain egg and are a little higher in fat. Rice noodles are slightly softer in texture and lower in protein than wheat noodles and cellophane or transparent noodles are made from ground mung beans.

Stir-fries & soups

Noodles are a good low-fat accompaniment to a stir-fry, taking only a few minutes to cook while you stir the vegetables and flavourings in the wok. They are also ideal added to a home-made vegetable or chicken broth.

Quick savoury noodles

Dried savoury noodles in a variety of flavours are becoming increasingly popular. Just add boiling water for a quick and tasty snack or light meal.

FOOD	FAT g	FIBRE g	CARB g	ENERGY kcal	ENERGY kJ
MIXED VEGETABLES					
frozen, boiled, 100 g	0.5	++	7	42	180
MOLASSES					
1 tbsp	0	0	10	40	167
MULBERRIES					
cooked with sugar, 100 g	0	1.2	16	65	276
cooked without sugar, 100 g	0	1.3	7	30	129
raw, 100 g	0	1.5	8	36	152
MUSHROOMS					
Chinese, dried, raw, 25 g	0.4	++	15	71	297
closed/open cup, boiled, 100 g	0.3	2.3	0.4	11	48
closed/open cup, fried, 50 g	8	1.5	0	79	323
closed/open cup, raw, 100 g	0.5	2.3	0.4	13	55
oyster, raw, 100 g	0.2	++	0	8	35
straw, canned, 100 g	0.2	++	1.2	15	62
MUSTARD					
American, 1 tsp, 5 g	0.2	++	0.1	3	12
English, powder, 1 tsp	0.9	++	1	14	57
English, powder, made up, heaped tsp, 8g	1.4	++	1	23	94
French, 1 tsp, 5 g	0.2	++	0.2	4	16
wholegrain, retail, 14 g	1.4	++	1	20	82
MUSTARD & CRESS					
raw, 5 g portion	0	0.2	0	1	3
NASHI PEAR					
1 raw, 130 g	0.1	++	9	38	159
NECTARINE					
raw, 1, 150 g (weight with stone)	0.2	3.3	14	60	257
NOODLES					
egg, boiled, 100 g	0.5	1.0	13	62	264
noodles, fried, 100 g	12	0.9	11	153	638
plain, boiled, 100 g	0.4	1.2	13	62	264
plain, dried, 100 g	6	5.2	76	388	1646
rice, cooked, 100 g	1.9	1.1	18	95	405
rice, dried, 100 g	0.1	++	82	360	1506
NUTS					
almonds, shelled, 2, 13 g	7	1.7	1	80	329
Brazil, shelled, 3, 10 g	7	0.8	0.3	68	281

ORANGES

Oranges, a popular citrus fruit, originated in China, but are now cultivated all over the world. They are relatively inexpensive and are an excellent source of vitamin C.

Nutritional content

One orange provides about 10 g of carbohydrate in the form of natural sugar. Oranges also contain some fibre and they have a high vitamin C content. All oranges are a good source of folate and carotene (vitamin A) with particularly high levels of carotene found in red blood oranges. Useful amounts of calcium and magnesium are present in both oranges and orange juice. Although oranges have a low iron content, the high vitamin C level helps the absorption of iron from other non-meat foods, especially eggs.

Vitamin C

The vitamin C content of fruit varies according to the season. This list shows the average Vitamin C content of a range of raw fruits measured per 100g:

apple, eating	5 mg
banana	11 mg
blackcurrants	200 mg
cherries	9 mg
grapefruit	36 mg
guava	230 mg
orange	54 mg
peach	31 mg

O

FOOD	FAT g	FIBRE g	CARB g	ENERGY kcal	kJ
(NUTS)					
cashew nuts, roasted/salted, 10, 10 g	5	++	2	61	253
chestnut purée, 100 g	2	3	27	133	560
chestnuts, peeled, 5, 50 g	1.4	3.0	18	85	360
cob (hazel) shelled, 10, 10 g	6	0.6	0.6	65	269
peanuts, dry roasted, 25 g	12	1.9	3	147	610
peanuts, roasted & salted, 25 g	13	1.7	2	151	623
pecans, shelled, 5, 30 g	21	++	2	207	853
pistachios, roasted/salted, 10 kernels, 10 g	6	++	1	60	249
pistachios, with shells, 25 g	8	++	1	83	343
walnuts, shelled, 6 halves, 20 g	14	1.2	1	138	567
OILS (see Fats & Oils)					
OKRA					
boiled, 50 g	0.4	2.0	1	14	60
canned, 50 g	++	1.4	1	8	32
raw, 100 g	1	4.5	3	31	130
OLIVES					
in brine, without stones, 50 g	6	2.0	0	52	211
in brine, 50 g (weight with stones)	4	1.6	0	41	169
ONIONS					
boiled, 100 g	0.1	0.7	3.7	17	73
fried, 40 g	5	1.3	6	66	274
pickled, 1, 15 g	0	0.2	1	4	15
raw, 1 medium, 150 g	0.3	2.3	12	54	225
ORANGES					
juice, fresh squeezed, 100 g	0	0.1	8	33	140
juice, unsweetened, 100 g	0.1	0.1	9	36	153
raw, 1 medium, peeled, 120 g	0.1	2.2	10	44	190
ORTANIQUE (see Mandarin Oranges)					
OXTAIL					
casseroled, meat only, 100 g	13	0	0	243	1014
casseroled, with fat & bones, 100 g	5	0	0	92	386
PANCAKES/CREPES)					
savoury, made with full-fat milk, 1, 60 g	11	0.6	14	164	683
savoury, made with skimmed milk, 1, 60 g	9	0.6	15	149	623
sweet, made with full-fat milk, 1, 60 g	10	0.5	21	181	756
sweet, made with skimmed milk, 1, 60 g	8	0.5	21	168	705

P

PASTA

Pasta, such as spaghetti, penne, linguini and fusilli is very popular as a quick, easy and tasty meal whatever the occasion. Most children like pasta and will be tempted by the different shapes.

Preparation

Pasta is a very useful basis for all types of dishes. It is naturally low in fat, however, some pasta dishes can be very high in fat especially if cheese or cream sauces are used.

Coloured pasta

Coloured pasta contains tomato purée, squid ink or spinach to give the typical colours. It may have a slightly higher fibre content than white pasta.

Most pasta is made from durum wheat and has a similar nutritional content regardless of shape, containing B group vitamins, some fibre and iron. Wholemeal pasta is higher in fibre and iron than white varieties. Fresh pasta contains more water than dried, but otherwise there is very little nutritional difference.

P

FOOD	FAT g	FIBRE g	CARB g	ENERGY kcal	kJ
PAPADUM					
fried, 1, 13 g	2	1.2	5	48	201
raw, 1, 13 g	0.2	1.5	6	35	150
PARSNIP					
boiled, 65 g	1	2.9	8	43	181
raw, 100g	1	4.3	13	64	271
PASSION FRUIT					
raw, 1, 15 g	0.1	++	1	5	23
PASTA					
buckwheat pasta, dried, 100 g	2	4.8	74	352	1484
capaleti, prosciutto-filled, fresh, boiled 150g	50	4	8	354	1492
fusilli, tricolore, fresh, boiled, 210g	59	4	5	363	1536
corn pasta, dried, 100 g	2	3.2	82	367	1549
lasagne, fresh, 100 g	1.4	1.8	28	147	624
linguine, dried, boiled, 210 g	1.5	2.3	66	321	1363
macaroni, boiled, 150 g	0.8	2.3	28	129	548
macaroni, canned in cheese sauce, 335 g	22	2.7	55	462	1940
macaroni cheese bake, 300 g	32	2.4	41	534	2229
penne, fresh, 100 g	1.6	2.1	30	159	675
potato gnocchi, fresh, 100 g	0.3	0.4	37	170	724
ravioli, fresh, mushroom & ricotta, 100 g	7	1.8	26	194	81
spaghetti, white, boiled, 220 g	2	4.0	49	229	972
spaghetti, white, 100 g	2	5.1	74	342	1456
spaghetti, wholemeal, boiled, 220 g	2	8.8	51	249	1067
tagliatelli, fresh, with sun-dried tomato, 100 g	1.4	1.4	24	125	531
tortellini, spinach & ricotta, fresh, boiled 150g	47	6	8	323	1361
PASTA SAUCES					
bacon & tomato (amatriciana), fresh, 100 g	5	1.4	7	90	374
bolognese, fresh, 100 g	7.2	1.6	6	119	498
carbonara, fresh, 100 g	12	0	9	175	729
carbonara, jar, 100 g	13	0	3	145	599
four cheese, fresh, 100 g	11	0.5	6	149	62
four cheese, low-fat, fresh, 100 g	4	0.2	6	80	335
smoky bacon, long-life, 100 g	13	++	7	165	685
spicy pepperoni, long-life, 100 g	12	++	8	147	608
tomato & basil, rich, jar, 100 g	6	0.8	8	90	373
tomato & mascarpone, fresh, 100 g	8	0.4	9	118	491

P

PEAS

Both fresh and frozen peas are good sources of minerals and vitamins. The nutritional content of fresh peas is highest immediately after picking. Frozen peas can be compared nutritionally with freshly picked peas, and may have a higher vitamin content than fresh pods, which have been stored for some time. Quick to prepare, peas are one of the most popular accompaniments to a main meal.

Vitamins and minerals

The vitamin C content in peas is not very high, but they are a good source of carotene (vitamin A) The fibre content of peas is high, particularly for small peas, which have a high proportion of skin to flesh.

Mangetout and sugar snap peas have a similar nutritional content to fresh podded peas. These sweeter-tasting varieties are eaten whole and are equally delicious raw in salads or stir-fried in Thai or Chinese dishes.

P

FOOD	FAT g	FIBRE g	CARB g	ENERGY kcal	kJ
(PASTA SAUCES)					
tomato & olive (puttanesca), jar, 100g	6	0.9	7	90	375
pesto, green, jar, 100 g	44	2	4	430	1770
pesto, red, jar, 100 g	32	2	5	321	1325
PASTRY					
choux, cooked, 100 g	20	1.4	30	325	1355
filo, raw, 10 sheets, 100 g	4	0.8	62	315	1317
flaky, cooked, 100 g	41	2.1	46	560	2332
shortcrust, cooked, 100 g	32	2.5	54	521	2174
wholemeal, cooked, 100 g	33	6.0	45	499	2080
PÂ TÉ					
liver, 50 g	14	0	0.5	158	654
liver, low-fat, 50 g	6	0	1	96	398
smoked mackerel, 50 g	17	0	0.6	184	761
tuna, 50 g	9	0	0.2	118	491
vegetable, 50 g	7	++	3	87	359
PEACHES					
canned in juice, 120 g	0	1.1	12	47	198
canned in syrup, 120 g	0	1.1	17	66	280
dried, 100 g	0.8	13	53	219	936
dried, cooked with sugar, 100 g	0.3	5.1	26	104	446
dried, cooked without sugar, 100 g	0.3	5.3	22	89	383
raw, with skin, 1 medium, 110 g	0.1	2.5	8	36	156
PEARS					
canned in juice, 135 g	0	2.0	12	45	190
canned in syrup, 135 g	0	2.0	18	68	290
cooked with sugar, 100 g	0.1	1.6	22	89	152
cooked without sugar, 100 g	0.1	1.8	9	35	152
dried, 100 g	0.5	11	52	207	884
raw, with peel,1 , 150 g	1.5	4.7	11	83	344
PEAS					
frozen, boiled, 70 g	0.6	5.1	7	48	204
mushy, canned, 80 g	0.6	++	11	65	276
raw, shelled, 100 g	1.5	4.7	11	83	344
split, dried, boiled, 100 g	1	4.6	23	126	538

P

POTATOES

Potatoes, 'the treasure of the Incas', are very familiar to us now, but were not accepted as a staple food in Europe until well into the 18th century. Once established the humble potato quickly became a major food source for millions of people.

Potato types

The many different varieties of potatoes fall into two major groups, floury and waxy. There is very little difference in nutritional content between them, but floury potatoes are better for roasting, mashing and frying while the waxy varieties are best for steaming, boiling and using in salads.

Chips (fries)

Deep-fried potato chips are perhaps the most popular form of serving and eating this tuber. The fat content of chips varies – thin French fries have a larger surface area to content, so contain more fat per 100g. Thick cut chips are slightly lower in fat and oven chips contain the least.

Nutritional content

This is mostly starch, but because of the comparatively large amounts eaten, potatoes contribute more fibre, protein, iron and vitamin C to the diet than most other vegetables. Vitamin C is stored near the skin, so potatoes are best left unpeeled or peeled very thinly.

FOOD	FAT g	FIBRE g	CARB g	ENERGY kcal	ENERGY kJ
PEPPERS					
green, raw, 1 , 160 g	0.5	3	4	24	104
red, raw, 1 , 160 g	0.6	3	10	51	214
yellow, raw, 1 , 160 g	0.3	3.2	9	42	181
PHEASANT					
roast, meat only, 100 g	9	0	0	213	892
PIGEON					
roast, meat only, 1, 115 g	15	0	0	265	1105
PINEAPPLE					
canned in juice, 1 ring/6 chunks, 40 g	0	0.3	5	19	80
canned in syrup, 1 ring/ 6 chunks, 40 g	0	0.3	7	26	109
dried, 100 g	1.3	8.8	68	276	2190
raw, 1 slice, without skin, 80 g	0.2	1	8	33	141
PLANTAIN (see Banana)					
PLUMS					
canned in juice, with stones, 200 g	0	2	21	80	336
canned in syrup, with stones, 200 g	0	2	31	118	506
damson, raw, 100 g	0	3.7	10	38	16
damson, cooked with sugar, 100 g	0	3.0	19	74	316
damson, cooked without sugar, 100 g	0	3.4	9	34	147
raw, without stones, 55 g	0.1	1.2	5	19	80
raw, 100 g (weight with stones)	0.1	2.2	8	34	145
POMEGRANATE					
flesh only, raw, 100 g	0.6	++	17	72	301
PORK					
crackling, cooked, 25 g	11	0	0	138	570
fillet, sliced, lean only, grilled, 100 g	4	0	0	170	719
leg, roasted, lean only, 90 g	6	0	0	167	699
loin chop, grilled, lean only, 100 g	11	0	0	226	945
POTATOES					
baked, flesh/skin, 1, 180 g	0.4	++	57	245	1046
boiled, 1, 60 g	0.1	0.8	10	43	184
chips, oven, baked, 10 chips, 100 g	4	2.8	30	162	687
chips, thin fries, takeaway, 110 g	17	3.4	37	308	1291
chips, thick, takeaway, 10 chips, 100 g	12	3	31	239	1001
mashed, with butter/milk, 175 g	8	2.3	27	182	767

R

READY MEALS & PREPARED FOODS

An essential feature of today's busy lifestyle, convenience foods have been with us for a long time – canned foods have been available since the beginning of the twentieth century, while frozen and chilled dishes are hugely popular.

Nutritional value

Most households will have a small stock of cans, such as baked beans, spaghetti hoops, sardines or tuna, fruit and vegetables. These storecupboard foods are useful in an emergency but it should be remembered that their nutritional value will always be lower than foods which are fresh or frozen.

Choices

We are able to buy a huge array of ready-to-cook chilled and frozen foods and dishes. Used sensibly, these are a great way to keep a busy household fed. However, they cannot replace freshly cooked foods and it is wise to check labels carefully for nutritional value. A person of normal weight needs a main meal that will provide not less than 500 calories.

FOOD	FAT g	FIBRE g	CARB g	ENERGY kcal	kJ
(POTATOES)					
new, boiled, with skin, 1, 40 g	0.1	0.6	6	26	112
new, boiled, without skin, 1, 40 g	0.1	0.5	7	30	128
roasted, 1 , 85 g	4	2	22	127	536
PRUNES					
canned in juice, without stones, 100 g	0.2	++	20	79	335
canned in syrup, with stones, 100 g	0.2	++	23	90	386
cooked with sugar, 100 g	0.2	7	26	103	439
cooked with sugar, with stones, 100 g	0.2	6.3	24	95	405
cooked without sugar, 100 g	0.3	7.4	20	81	346
cooked without sugar, with stones, 100 g	0.2	6.7	18	74	314
ready-to-eat, 100 g	0.3	11	29	121	514
PUMPKIN					
boiled, 100 g	0.3	0.5	2	13	56
raw, 100 g	0.2	0.5	2	13	55
QUICHE					
Lorraine, (cream, bacon, cheese), 100 g	28	0.8	20	390	1629
Lorraine, wholemeal pastry,100 g	28	2.0	17	384	1599
mushroom, 100 g	20	1.2	18	284	1185
mushroom, wholemeal pastry, 100 g	20	2.3	15	277	1156
RABBIT					
casseroled, meat only, 100 g	8	0	0	179	749
RADISH					
red, raw, 3, 24 g	0	0.2	0.5	3	12
white (mooli), raw, 100 g	0.1	++	4	24	100
RAISINS (see Dried Fruit)					
RASPBERRIES					
canned in syrup, 90 g	0.1	4	20	79	337
cooked with sugar, 100 g	0.3	6	15	63	271
cooked without sugar, 100 g	0.3	6.5	4	24	105
frozen, raw 100 g	0.3	7	5	26	110
raw, 60 g	0.2	4	3	15	65
READY MEALS/PREPARED FOODS					
bhaji, onion, 1, 140 g	30	10	31	435	1814
bhaji, vegetable, 1, 140 g	21	6.3	30	329	1365
beef casserole, canned, 200 g	5	1.6	13	146	614
burger, spicy bean, 1, cooked, quarter-pounder	13	3.4	27	241	1010

READY MEALS & PREPARED FOODS

Complete meals can be bought frozen or chilled and are very useful if you lack time. However, it is worth checking whether some dishes may be cheaper and as easy to make at home.

in jars or in long-life packs. Check for fat content – sauces based on cheese or mascarpone will be high in fat while tomato-based sauces should be lower. Freshly grated Parmesan cheese is the traditional enhancement for pasta, but will also increase the fat content. For more balance and nutrition, add frozen or freshly prepared and cooked vegetables such as peppers, mushrooms, spinach or tomatoes to your pasta dish or serve with a salad.

Pasta sauces

Pasta cooks quickly, so cook it yourself, but choose a ready-made pasta sauce to add to it. Pasta sauces can be bought fresh chilled,

FOOD	FAT g	FIBRE g	CARB g	ENERGY kcal	kJ
(READY MEALS/PREPARED FOODS)					
burger, vegetarian, 1, 47 g	4	0.9	12	95	400
cannelloni, spinach & ricotta, 450 g	35	2.3	58	662	2768
cashew nut roast mix, 100 g	32	++	26	480	2000
chicken chow mein, 340 g	7	6.5	49	353	1493
chicken kiev, 1, 140 g	35	1.3	14	427	1769
chicken kiev, reduced fat, 1, 140 g	20	1.7	16	319	1330
chicken pie, individual, baked, 130 g	23	3	32	374	1563
chicken & turkey satay, 1 stick, 30 g	3	0.4	0.8	45	188
chilli con carne, 220 g	19	7	18	332	1390
chow mein, 100 g	3.4	0.6	16	119	503
cod fillet, breaded, 1 fillet, 170 g	13	3	24	304	1280
cod fish cake, 1, 90 g	8	0.7	15	168	703
cod mornay, with cheese sauce, 180 g	14	1.4	3	236	987
corned beef hash, canned, 200 g	18	++	12	328	6871
cottage pie, 350 g	14	3.5	35	315	1322
egg fried rice, 100 g	2.2	1.1	25	149	682
falafel, 6, 85 g	7	7	16	200	829
fish pie, 100 g	4	0.9	9	93	389
garlic bread, half baguette, 90 g	16	2.0	41	342	1434
garlic bread, half baguette, reduced-fat, 90 g	8	1.8	41	263	1109
gefilte fish balls, 6, 100 g	3.9	1.0	12	140	585
hash browns, 100 g	7.3	++	24	174	729
Lancashire hotpot, 450 g	16	5.4	46	424	1784
lasagne, meat, 100 g	9	1.4	10	161	675
spinach, wholemeal, 100 g	3	3	13	193	395
lasagne, vegetable, 100 g	5	0.5	14	212	517
macaroni cheese, canned, 200 g	9.5	0.6	20	191	799
noodle, Thai-style, 100 g	6	0.8	16	142	598
noodle/pasta savoury pots,					
dry weight before reconstituting					
chicken curry, 87 g	14	3.2	56	384	1610
chilli, 71 g	14	1.7	47	337	1409
korma, 75 g	3	1.1	52	273	1148
mushroom & chicken, 68 g	8	2.7	43	269	1133
spicy curry, 119 g	20	4.4	77	530	2229
nut roast, dry mix, 100 g	30	7.0	23	482	2011

R

READY MEALS & PREPARED FOODS

One advantage of ready meals and prepared foods is that most of them can be heated quickly in the microwave. This is a great boon for busy people, especially in a family where everybody seems to have conflicting schedules!

dishes or thawed frozen food reaches the correct temperature, otherwise it won't be properly cooked.

For a meal in minutes that combines fresh with ready-made food use the microwave to bake a potato to go with your shop-bought salad or quiche. Simply prick the potato with a knife and cook it on Full Power for 6 minutes, turning once. Leave the potato to stand for 10 minutes, then it's ready to eat.

Microwave cooking

Microwaving is an excellent and safe way to reheat or cook food, but it is very important to make sure that ready-prepared chilled

FOOD	FAT g	FIBRE g	CARB g	ENERGY kcal	kJ
(READY MEALS/PREPARED FOODS)					
pasta shapes in tomato sauce, can, 205 g	0.8	1.2	26	128	542
pasta shapes with sausage, can, 213 g	11	0.4	26	230	967
pasty, cheese & onion, 1, 150 g	33	1.5	35	477	1988
pasty, meat & potato (Cornish), 1, 227 g	36	2.5	43	567	2367
pizza, deep-pan, pepperoni, 190 g	21	5.6	45	453	1900
pizza, thin & crispy, four cheese, 145 g	13	4.3	40	343	1443
pizza, thin & crispy, ham/mushroom, 160 g	11	7.6	30	288	1211
potato, jacket, cheese & beans, 340 g	7	7.5	47	305	1286
potato, jacket, chilli con carne, 340 g	12	4.1	35	319	1341
potato, jacket, tuna & sweetcorn, 340 g	13	3.4	43	333	1398
potato skins					
cheese & bacon, 140 g	22	3.5	24	349	1445
spicy with salsa, 205 g	8	0.8	47	290	165
prawn cocktail, (prawns & mayonnaise), 100 g	35	0.5	3	353	1457
prawn cocktail, reduced-fat, 100 g	13	0.5	3	160	662
raita, yogurt, cucumber & mint, 65 g	1.2	++	6	41	180
ravioli, meat, canned in tomato sauce, 200 g	2.3	1.1	26	145	613
salmon fish cakes, oven-baked, 2, 140 g	15	2.2	26	306	1280
samosa, meat, 1 large, 140 g	79	3.4	25	830	3430
samosa, vegetable, 1 large, 140 g	59	3.4	31	660	2736
sauce, cooking					
black bean, 100 g	0.6	0.8	18	80	340
hoisin, 100 g	2	0.7	37	175	740
korma, 100 g	14	1	11	180	740
madras, 100 g	8	2	10	115	480
red wine, 100 g	0.6	0+	10	46	195
sauce, cooking for chicken					
extra creamy mushroom, 100 g	7	0.5	9	87	362
honey & mustard, 100 g	5	0.6	15	106	443
sauce, stir-fry sachet					
black bean, 100 g	11	1.5	17	185	765
green Thai, 100 g	32	2.1	12	345	1415
oyster & spring onion, 100 g	0.7	1.1	20	92	391
sausage roll, flaky pastry,1 medium, 60 g	22	0.7	19	286	1191
sausage roll, shortcrust pastry, 1, 60 g	19	0.8	23	275	1149
sausage roll, vegetarian, 1 roll, 50 g	8	0.8	12	267	1115

RICE

Rice is a major staple carbohydrate for a large sector of the world's population. It is low in fat and a good source of B vitamins, although brown rice is better than white rice.

Nutritional content

Weight for weight rice is lower in protein and calories than bread and wheat flour. Rice contains B group vitamins and is a source of calcium, iron, zinc and other minerals and vitamins, but in quite low levels. Much of the B vitamin and mineral content of rice is in the outer husk of the grain, but some of this is lost in the polishing process. Although there are a number of different varieties of rice, there is very little nutritional difference between them.

Types of rice

Long-grain rice is used for most savoury dishes, with basmati rice particularly prized for its flavour. Short-grain round rice, used for savoury dishes in Thailand and China, is also the rice of choice for puddings. The Italian arborio rice has a starchy, glutinous quality good in risottos.

FOOD	FAT g	FIBRE g	CARB g	ENERGY kcal	kJ
(READY MEALS/PREPARED FOODS)					
Scotch egg, retail, 1, 120 g	21	1.9	16	301	1255
shepherd's pie, 100 g	4	1	10	90	378
spaghetti bolognese, can, 200 g	2.7	1.0	26	149	692
spaghetti rings in tomato sauce, can, 200 g	0.4	1.1	23	111	472
spaghetti with sausages, can in tomato sauce, 200 g	5.2	1.0	22	165	694
spring roll, vegetable, 1, 140 g	9	2.3	37	250	1055
steak & kidney pie, puff pastry, 150 g	24	1.4	40	423	1769
steak & kidney pie, shortcrust pastry, 240 g	42	3.4	55	715	2986
sweet & sour pork, canned, 200 g	2.6	2.0	28	206	868
tortellini, fresh, meat, 100 g	6	1.4	21	170	710
tortellini, fresh, spinach & ricotta, 100 g	4.8	2.4	24	169	712
vegetarian fillets, mycoprotein, 1, 100 g	1.8	4.7	6	90	381
vegetarian fillets, mycoprotein, garlic & herb, 1, 100 g	10	4.1	17	198	828
vine leaves, stuffed, vegetarian, 1, 30 g	1.5	++	7	44	184
REDCURRANTS					
jelly, 1 tsp, 9 g	0	0	6	22	92
raw, 100 g	0	++	4	21	89
cooked with sugar, 100 g	0	5.8	13	53	227
cooked without sugar, 100 g	0	6.3	4	17	76
RHUBARB					
canned in syrup, 100 g	0	1.3	8	31	130
raw, 100 g	0.1	2.3	0.8	7	32
cooked with sugar, 140 g	0.1	2.8	16	67	284
cooked without sugar, 140 g	0.1	2.1	0.7	7	30
RICE					
arborio, raw, 100 g	0.5	0.5	79	349	1481
basmati, boiled, 100 g	0.3	0.8	30	123	522
brown, boiled, 180 g	2.0	2.7	58	254	1075
red (wild), raw, 100 g	2.7	2.5	73	343	1453
white, easy-cook, boiled, 180 g	2	1.8	56	248	1057
white, polished, boiled, 180 g	0.5	1.4	53	221	940
RICECAKES					
plain, 1 slice	0.2	0.1	6	28	120
rice & maize, with cheese, 1, 10 g	0.3	0.1	8	38	160

S

SEEDS & NUTS

Most nuts and seeds contain protein, fat and carbohydrate to a greater or lesser degree, depending on the type. In most seeds the fat is poly- or monounsaturated.

Vitamins & minerals

Seeds are high in fibre and may be a good source of minerals, B vitamins and vitamin E, relative to the quantities eaten. For example, 100 g of sesame seeds contains about 600 mg of calcium, but a teaspoon of sesame seeds weighs less than 5g. Milk, at 115 g calcium per 100 g, is easier to include in the diet.

Calorie content

The nutritional value of nuts and seeds makes them a useful part of a vegetarian diet. However, they make a very high calorie snack. For example, a small packet of roasted peanuts contains about 20 g fat which is 300 calories.

FOOD	FAT g	FIBRE g	CARB g	ENERGY kcal	kJ
SALSIFY					
boiled, 100 g	0.4	++	9	23	99
SATSUMA (see Mandarin Oranges)					
SAUCES/SAVOURY					
bread, whole milk, 45 g	2.3	0.3	6	50	208
bread, semi-skimmed milk, 45 g	1.4	0.3	6	42	177
brown, bottled, 20 g	0	++	5	20	84
cheese, whole milk, 100 g	15	0.2	9	197	819
cheese, semi-skimmed milk, 100 g	13	0.2	9	179	750
hollandaise, 50 g	38	++	0	358	1456
horseradish, 20 g	1.7	++	4	31	128
tartare, jar, 20 g	4	0.2	4	58	242
tomato ketchup, bottled, 20 g	0	++	5	20	84
white, whole milk, 100 g	11	0.3	10	150	624
white, semi-skimmed,100 g	11	0.3	8	128	539
Worcestershire, 15 g	0	0	2	10	41
SAUSAGE					
beef, fried or grilled, 1, 40 g	7	0.3	6	108	450
black pudding, dry-fried, 1 slice, 30 g	6	0.2	5	89	371
black pudding, fried in oil, 1 slice, 30 g	7	0.5	4	310	381
bratwurst, 1, 75 g	16	++	2	195	811
chicken frankfurters, 3, 100 g	21	0	6	243	1007
chorizo, 1, 60 g	15	0	1	182	757
liver sausage, 100 g	17	0.5	6	226	942
mortadella, 100 g	30	++	1	331	1368
pork, fried, 1, 40 g	10	0.3	4	128	527
pork, grilled, 1, 40 g	13	0.4	6	165	686
salami, 1 slice, 20 g	9	0	0.4	98	406
salami stick, 1, 25 g	12	0	0.4	132	547
vegetarian, raw, 1, 35 g	5	0.4	3	88	366
SEEDS					
melon, 15 g	7	++	3	87	365
poppy, 15 g	4	++	2	46	195
pumpkin, 15 g	7	++	2	85	354
sesame, 15 g	9	++	0.1	90	371
sunflower, 15 g	7	++	3	87	362
sunflower, toasted, 15 g	7	++	3	90	375

SOUPS

A soup can be a thin broth or a hearty meal. Home-made lentil and vegetable soup is low in fat, cheap and easy to make. Served with bread, it makes a good filling meal on a winter's day.

Stock

The basis for soup is often a stock, made by cooking vegetables or meat or fish bones with seasoning and herbs and straining off the resulting liquor. The stock gives the soup its flavour. Try to use home-made stock rather than stock cubes, which have little nutritional content and tend to be high in salt.

Ready-made soups

The most nutritious soups are probably those made at home from freshly prepared produce. However, a wide variety of soups can be bought canned, dried or fresh-chilled which are perfect for a snack or meal. Remember to check the label for salt content and to see how much protein and energy one portion provides.

FOOD	FAT g	FIBRE g	CARB g	ENERGY kcal	kJ
SHARON FRUIT					
raw, 100 g	0	++	19	73	311
SNACKS					
bacon-flavoured maize snacks, 25 g	6	1.2	12	117	490
banana chips, 25 g	8	1.2	15	128	534
cheese-flavoured biscuits, 50 g	14	1.3	27	257	1074
corn chips (tortilla), 100 g	19	4	68	461	1935
croûtons, flavoured, 50 g	15	1.3	26	260	1083
fruit & nut mix with coconut, 100 g	15	++	54	374	1572
peanuts & raisins, 25 g	7	1.7	9	109	455
potato chips (matchstick-style), 50 g	17	1.9	27	264	1102
potato crisps, bag, 34.5 g	12	1.4	17	183	759
potato crisps, low-fat, 28 g	6	1.4	17	130	543
potato rings, 25 g	5	0.8	17	117	492
prawn crackers, 100 g	31	0.4	60	534	2231
pretzels, 50 g	2	1.7	41	200	850
spicy maize, gram & peanut mix, 100 g	34	6	51	546	2278
spicy rice cracker mix, 100 g	0.1	1.6	83	360	1525
vegetable (not potato) crisps, 100 g	27	6	37	407	1691
SOFT DRINKS					
blackcurrant cordial, diluted, 250 ml	0	0	20	75	323
blackcurrant cordial, low sugar, diluted, 250 ml	0	0	1	8	35
elderflower, concentrated, 10 ml	0	0	6	24	102
fruit drink/squash, concentrated, 50 ml	0	0	12	47	200
fruit squash, diluted, 250 ml	0	0	1.3	8	35
fruit squash, no added sugar, diluted, 250 ml	0	0	0.1	4	16
lime juice, undiluted, 45ml	0	0	13	50	216
cola type, canned, 333 ml	0	0	35	133	559
diet (light) cola, canned, 333 ml	0	0	1	1	4
diet (light) lemonade, canned, 333 ml	0	0	1	4	13
ginger beer, canned, 333 ml	0	0	25	110	462
lemonade, canned, 333 ml	0	0	36	141	595
orangeade, canned, 333 ml	0	0	43	172	724
SOUPS					
carrot & coriander, ready-made, 300 ml	4	1.8	10	105	441
condensed, chicken, undiluted, 150 g	11	++	9	147	611
condensed, tomato, undiluted, 150 g	10	++	22	185	771

S

SPINACH

Spinach is very nutritious and can be eaten as a vegetable accompaniment or added to dishes for colour. Once picked, spinach wilts quickly, so when buying choose leaves that are dark green.

Nutritional content

Spinach is a good source of fibre and contains more protein than some vegetables. It is high in carotene and folate and is a source of other B vitamins. Despite the popular myth spinach is low in iron and while its calcium content is high, neither is well absorbed.

Cooking spinach

Wash spinach thoroughly and remove any thick stalks and withered leaves. Maximise vitamins by cooking spinach in a steamer, or by cooking it in a microwave. Spinach can be boiled in a little water in a large saucepan and usually takes less than 5 minutes to cook. However, valuable vitamins will be lost when you throw the excess water away.

In very large quantities the high oxalate content of spinach may be the cause of renal stones in some people.

FOOD	FAT g	FIBRE g	CARB g	ENERGY kcal	kJ
(SOUPS)					
corn chowder, ready-made, 300 ml	7	4	25	183	771
cream of chicken, canned, 150 g	6	++	7	87	363
cream of mushroom, ready-made, 150 g	6	++	6	80	333
cream of tomato, ready-made, 150 g	5	++	9	83	345
lentil soup, canned, 100 g	0.2	++	7	39	164
mushroom, ready-made, 300 ml	9	0.9	11	153	633
powder, rehydrated, 200 ml	3.4	++	16	96	408
powder, reduced calorie, rehydrated to 250 ml	2	0.3	9	59	248
reduced calorie soup, canned, 150 g	0.3	++	6	30	131
SPINACH					
fresh, boiled, 90 g	0.7	3	1	17	71
frozen, boiled, 90 g	0.7	3	0.4	19	81
raw, 100 g	0.8	4	2	25	103
SPREADS/SAVOURY					
barbecued bean paste, 100 g	0.4	++	20	106	449
chicken & mushroom, 100 g	11	++	5	187	782
peanut butter, on bread, 16 g	9	1.1	2	100	413
salmon, 100 g	10	++	5	172	720
sandwich spread, 1 tbsp, 16 g	2	++	4	30	124
soya with herbs & chives, 100 g	28	++	6	290	1210
SPRING GREENS					
boiled, 100 g	0.7	3.4	2	20	82
raw, 100 g	1.0	6.1	3	33	136
SPRING ONIONS					
raw, 1, 10 g	0.1	++	0.3	2	10
SPROUTING BEANS					
alfalfa, raw, 100 g	1	++	0.4	24	100
mung bean, 100 g	0.2	++	6	35	146
SQUASH					
acorn, baked, 70 g	0.1	++	9	39	164
butternut, baked, 70 g	0.1	++	5	22	96
spaghetti, baked, 70 g	0.2	++	3	16	67
STAR FRUIT (CARAMBOLA)					
raw, 100 g	0.3	1.7	7	32	136
STOCK CUBES					
any, 1 cube, 5 g	0.8	0	0.5	12	52

TOFU

Tofu is made from soya beans and is very useful in the vegetarian diet as a source of protein and a basis for many dishes. Most tofu has a high calcium and magnesium content, although some varieties may have lower levels depending on the processing method. Tofu also provides some B vitamins and some iron and zinc. The fat content is fairly low in relation to the protein content.

Different varieties

Tofu is available in various forms. It can be soft and creamy or in varying degrees of firmness. Smoked and flavoured tofu is also available for people who find plain tofu bland.

Serving suggestion

Add tofu to vegetable soups or slice smoked tofu into a pasta sauce. It is also delicious served as a dip flavoured with garlic and lemon juice.

FOOD	FAT g	FIBRE g	CARB g	ENERGY kcal	ENERGY kJ
STRAWBERRIES					
canned in juice, 100 g	0	1.0	12	50	211
canned in syrup, 100 g	0	0.9	17	65	279
strawberries, raw, 100 g	0.1	2	6	27	113
STUFFING					
sage & onion, 50 g	7	1.2	10	116	481
SUET (see Fats and Oils)					
SUGAR					
any, 1 tsp, 5g	0	0	5	20	84
SUGAR SNAP PEAS					
boiled, 100 g	0.3	++	5	33	139
raw, 100 g	0.2	++	5	34	145
SULTANAS (see Dried Fruit)					
SWEDE					
boiled, 60 g	0.1	0.7	1	7	28
swede, raw, 100 g	0.3	2.4	5	24	101
SWEETCORN (see Corn)					
SWEET POTATO					
boiled, 65 g	0.2	1.4	13	55	233
sweet potato, raw, 100 g	0.3	2.3	21	87	372
SWISS CHARD (see Chard)					
TAHINI					
1 heaped tbsp, 19 g	11	++	0.2	115	477
TAMARILLOS (TREE TOMATO)					
raw, 90 g	0.3	++	4	25	108
TANGERINES (see Mandarin Oranges)					
TAPIOCA					
raw, 100 g	0.1	++	95	359	1531
boiled in water, 265g	0	0.3	19	75	315
TARAMASALATA (see Dips)					
TOFU					
canned, braised 100 g	19	0.1	7	247	1033
canned, fried, 100 g	25	++	4	302	1264
tofu, organic, 100 g	5	++	1	98	409
smoked, 100 g	7	++	2	127	530
steamed, 100 g	4	0.3	0.7	73	304

TURKEY

Many of us think of eating turkey only at Christmas or other celebrations, but this low-fat meat is available all year round: whole, in portions or cooked. As well as having most of its fat content in the skin, turkey is rich in B vitamins and zinc which helps to maintain a healthy immune system.

Light and dark meat

Light turkey meat (breast) has a fat content of less than 2 g/100 g raw weight, and dark meat (leg & thigh) contains nearly 4 g/100 g. Even dark meat has a fat content which is half that of beef or lamb.

SERVING SUGGESTIONS
Use cooked sliced turkey for sandwiches and salads, raw turkey meat to make sweet and sour dishes or delicious low-fat casseroles with vegetables.

FOOD	FAT g	FIBRE g	CARB g	ENERGY kcal	kJ
TOMATO					
cherry, raw, 100 g	0.4	1.3	3	18	76
juice, large glass, 250 ml	0	++	8	35	155
peeled, whole, canned, 400 g	0.4	3.2	12	64	276
puree, 1 heaped tbsp, 25 g	0.1	++	3	17	73
raw, 1, 85 g	0.3	1.1	3	14	62
sun-dried, 1, 10 g	5	++	0.5	50	204
sun-dried in oil, 100 g	51	0.8	4	93	2040
TORTILLAS					
wheat flour, 1, 50 g	0.5	1.4	30	131	557
TURKEY					
breast fillet, grilled, 100 g	2	0	0	155	658
drumstick, roasted, with skin & bone, 180 g	11	0	0	241	1010
minced, casseroled, 100 g	7	0	0	176	739
roasted, dark meat, no skin, 100 g	4	0	0	148	624
roasted, light meat, no skin, 100 g	1.4	0	0	132	558
roll, 1 slice, 19 g	2	0	1	32	132
smoked, 100 g	1.3	0	0	107	447
strips, stir-fried, 100 g	4.5	0	0	164	692
thigh, casseroled, 100 g	8	0	0	181	760
TURNIP					
boiled, 1 medium, 60 g	0.1	1.2	1	7	31
turnip, raw, 100 g	0.3	2.5	5	23	98
TZATZIKI (see Dips)					
VEAL					
escalope/cutlet, in breadcrumbs, fried, 150 g	12	0.5	7	323	1356
escalope, meat, no coating, fried, 100 g	7	0	0	196	825
fillet, roast, 100 g	12	0	0	230	963
VENISON					
roast, 120 g	3	0	0	198	838
VINEGAR					
all varieties, 1tbsp, 15ml	0	0	0	4	16
VINE LEAVES					
in brine, 100 g	0	4.5	0.2	15	64
WAFFLES					
plain, 1, 35 g	6	0.7	14	117	490
potato, frozen, cooked, 1	4	++	14	117	379

YOGURT

Yogurt is made by fermenting warmed milk with bacteria. The nutritional content depends on the type of milk used and the fat content of the milk. All yogurt contains protein, calcium and some B vitamins. It has no fibre content unless fruit, nuts or cereal fibre is added.

Live yogurt

'Live' yogurt contains the active bacteria and may have a role in helping to replace or maintain the natural bacterial flora of the gut. This can be valuable following a stomach upset, for example.

Flavoured yogurts

Flavoured yogurts made from cow's milk may be made from full-fat or skimmed milk with fruit, honey or other flavourings. Sugar or a non-calorific sweetener is usually also added. Check the label before buying.

Other yogurts

Greek-style yogurt is thicker and the fat content may be higher. Yogurts made from sheep, goat or soya milk have a slightly different protein and fat content.

FOOD	FAT g	FIBRE g	CARB g	ENERGY kcal	kJ
WATER CHESTNUTS					
canned, 40 g	0	++	5	20	82
raw, 50 g	0.1	++	5	23	99
WATERCRESS					
fresh, 20 g	0.2	0.6	0	4	19
YAM					
baked, 100 g	0.4	4.9	38	153	651
boiled, 130 g	0.4	5	43	173	738
yam, raw, 100 g	0.3	3.7	28	114	488
YEAST					
bakers, compressed, 15 g	0.1	0.9	0	7	34
dried, sachet, 7 g	0.1	1.4	0	12	50
YEAST EXTRACT					
vegetable extract, 4 g	0	0.1	0.8	9	37
YOGURT					
drinking yogurt					
peach & mango, low-fat,100 g	0.1	0	14	58	241
strawberry, 100 g	1.2	0	15	81	342
live fermented skimmed milk drink, 65 ml	<0.1	0	12	50	209
full-fat milk, fruit, 125 g	4	++	20	131	551
full-fat milk, plain, 125 g	4	++	10	99	416
goat, full-fat milk, 125 g	5	0	5	79	329
Greek-style, cow, 125 g	11	0	3	144	596
Greek-style, sheep, 125 g	9	0	7	133	553
low-fat, flavoured, 125 g	1	++	22	113	480
low-fat, fruit, 125 g	1	++	22	113	478
low-fat, muesli/nut, 125 g	3	++	24	140	593
low-fat, plain, 125 g	1	0	9	70	295
thick & creamy, 150 g	8	0	28	206	864
YORKSHIRE PUDDING					
1, 50 g	5	0.5	12	104	437

ESSENTIAL VITAMINS & MINERALS

These are the main vitamins and minerals you need. A good varied diet should contain these and other vitamins and minerals required in much smaller amounts.

Vitamin A (Retinol)
- Helps vision in dim light and to maintain healthy skin and surface tissues. In excess it can be poisonous. Supplements should not be taken in pregnancy.
- Found in liver, fish oils, dairy produce and egg yolks.

B Vitamins
- All B vitamins are essential for enzyme systems and metabolism.
- **B1** THIAMIN Found in animal and vegetable foods, such as milk, offal, pork, eggs, vegetables, fruit, wholegrain cereals and fortified breakfast cereals. In the UK all flour except wholemeal is fortified with thiamin.
- **B2** RIBOFLAVIN Widely distributed in foods, especially of animal origin. Milk is a particularly important source for many people.
- **B3** NIACIN Found in cereals, meat, fish, dairy products.

Folate (folic acid)
- Essential for cell growth, especially in pregnancy. Deficiency may lead to a form of anaemia. Found in offal, yeast extract, green leafy vegetables.

Vitamin C (Ascorbic acid)
- Essential for healthy connective tissue. Deficiency results in bleeding gums etc.
- Found in vegetables and fruit, especially citrus fruits, guavas and blackcurrants.

Vitamin D (Cholecalciferol)
- Needed for the absorption of calcium into the blood and maintenance of bones. In children deficiency of Vitamin D leads to rickets, and in adults to osteomalacia.
- The main source is the action of sunlight on the skin and most people require no more than this. Natural dietary sources are all of animal origin, such as fish and animal livers and oils, fatty fish, butter, milk and eggs. It may be added to some foods as a supplement.

Calcium
- Essential for the maintenance of bones and connective tissue. Deficiency may accelerate osteoporosis.
- Milk, cheese and yogurt are best sources. Also occurs in fruits, vegetables and seeds. May be added to bread and flour.

Iron
- Essential for the prevention of anaemia.
- Present in a wide range of foods, especially proteins – meat and dairy foods.

Zinc
- Helps wound healing and enzyme activity.
- Present in a wide range of foods, especially proteins – meat and dairy foods.